Super King

MW01293721

SUPER KINGDOM ADMIN

7 COMPONENTS FOR SUCCESS

RAINAH DAVIS

Copyright © 2016 by Rainah Davis
ISBN-10: 0-9984271-1-X
ISBN-13: 978-0-9984271-1-9

Front Cover Design: Brittany Oliver
Interior Design: Lisa DeSpain
Project Management: StartWrite Staff | Caroline Simmons &
Jennifer Eiland
Editor/Publisher: G.C. Simmons Publishing

Contents

Dedication

To the Super Kingdom Admins who have supported me, followed me on Social Media, and given me your amazing feedback—this book is for you! I am forever grateful that God would use me to assist you in serving the men and women of God. Never, ever forget serving sets you up for supernatural favor for you and generations following you! You are vitally necessary in the kingdom of God! I pray that these pages will help you to activate your super kingdom admin powers and that God will give you strength for the journey ahead! Many are called, but few are chosen. You have been hand-selected by God for such a time as this; go forth and know that even when it is tough: greater is He that is within you than he that is in the world! Now, let's go!

Foreword

THERE IS A KEY ELEMENT WHICH IS VITAL TO THE STRENGTH AND SUCCESS OF EVERY MINISTRY AND ORGANIZATION. From Fortune 500 companies and businesses in every sector to major social media platforms and churches of every size, they all rely heavily on this essential element for the success of their operations. Where this element is strong and valued, it helps these organizations to flourish. And where this element is weak or ignored, organizations are undoubtedly subject to suffer. Do you know what this key element is? Are you picking up on where I'm going? Are you interested in progressing forward? Then let me encourage you for just a few minutes to think critically about the absolute essentiality of solid ADMINISTRATION.

If you're a ministry leader who is serious about success, you cannot ignore the significance of administration.

If you're a volunteer or staff admin in a church or organization, you cannot devalue the role you play in administration.

And if you're a market place leader or corporate exec who was privileged to have someone slip you a copy of *The Super Kingdom Admin,* you cannot put it down just yet because you think it's a "church book" that may be out-of-touch with your business context.

I assure you that your company admins and organizational culture can be greatly enhanced by the transcendent principles outlined in this book. So read on!

Perhaps you're an ambitious or maybe even a restless leader who wants to take your church, organization or team(s) to the next level. Or perhaps you're a progressive or even frustrated admin seeking to develop your administrative gift, talents and skill-sets. No matter where you land on that spectrum, I believe that it is no accident that you're reading these words right now. I am convinced through personal experience that often the gap between where we are and where we could, or want to be, is simply access to key information and subsequent application. And fortunately for you, my friend, you've stumbled onto an incredible gem of transformative information. And what happens next in your life or organization is entirely up to you.

The book you hold in your hands contains 7 powerful components for administrative success. I can personally attest to the impact of these components because they have served as a timely catalyst to better equip our admins and strengthen the entire administrative culture of our organization.

In the summer of 2014, I sat down and carefully evaluated the internal operations of our church. I realized that while our ministry was growing in Sunday attendance and community involvement, we had unknowingly neglected the administration necessary to manage that growth. We were investing time and resources in key areas and leaders, but were not making similar investments in our administration and administrators. Do you see the problem? That's like driving a nice vehicle and forgetting to get your oil changed. I bet you're familiar with that moment when you look up at the sticker and then look down at your meter and realize that you've gone way past your prescribed scheduled oil change…no? Well, I am familiar with that awakening moment if you, dear reader, are not.

Sadly, this is a common oversight in many churches, ministries, organizations, and companies where it is very easy to become so enamored with our "vehicles" that we neglect the "oil" necessary to keep that vehicle's engine running smoothly. In the business world, that neglect can affect your bottom line, customer service reputation, and reduce your repeat clientele. In the church world, that can cost us painful *drops* that translate into the tangible loss of men, women and whole families and can even damage those we have been called to reach, disciple, and care for to glory of Jesus. Some of them will never return to a church because of hurt linked to *administrative drops* and may even never give Jesus another look because some church failed them or they fell through the cracks. Now that's serious. Did you catch that last point? Did it resonate in your heart? Did that open your eyes just a little bit to the importance of solid administration? Good. That's just one of many sobering and power-packed principles you'll come across and probably highlight in *The Super Kingdom Admin.* I know, spoiler alert! I just wanted to give you an appetizer for the great meal that's coming.

It was these types of conversations I was having with a brilliant and highly gifted influencer in the summer of 2014, a person adept and well experienced in the arena of church and market-place administration. I was fully aware that in order for the organization I lead to push to the next level of quality ministry, it would take more than just good preaching, engaging worship, and creative initiatives and environments; it would take an investment in strengthening our systemic operations by investing in the personnel tasked with managing the unseen and critical essentials of our church organization.

So I challenged that influencer to gather her invaluable wealth of expertise and experiences and develop them into a transferable format that could be used to train administrators and equip organizations with tangible tools to enhance their administrative operations. That brilliant influencer's name is Rainah Davis. And that content became a training intensive called "The Super Kingdom Admin," first taught in November of 2014, at the Hilton Hotel in Atlanta, GA, to the entire Admin Team of Victory Church ATL, where I serve as Lead Pastor. It was some four hours of revolutionary teaching and training that deeply impacted all of our admins and shifted the administrative culture of our church. In fact, the intensive was so transformative and empowering that following the close of our training, I immediately notified several other pastors and strongly insisted that they fly Rainah in to put on "The Super Kingdom Admin" with their administrative teams as well. That led to some extra travel miles for Rainah and a couple other churches' benefiting from the principles contained in this book!

After seeing the impact of the trainings and hearing the testimonies and stories that were emerging from the admins who had been exposed to Rainah's material, she was inspired again to go a step further when our talks led to her expanding and developing the training into the powerful book you now hold in your hands, *The Super Kingdom Admin*. In my estimation, it may become one of the most sought after works for church and market-place organizations seeking to fortify and advance their administrative culture and personnel and a timeless resource for admins in various contexts and capacities. The value of its practical applications and time-tested truths cannot be overstated in words. My only regret is that I did not have Rainah come to share with us sooner.

It is my great privilege and honor to pen this foreword and introduce this literary work to you by my good friend Rainah Davis. More than an experienced administrator and practitioner of the principles outlined in this book, she is a successful business woman, passionate communicator, and prolific author and ghost-writer, whose pronounced wisdom and extraordinary gifts and insights will no doubt make her a sought-after voice in the Body of Christ; a standout leader among our generation's key influencers; and one of your favorite authors! Rainah is an exceptional, creative mind.

Therefore, if you're an admin who is working or serving in any capacity, set yourself up to be a standout administrator by studying and applying the principles of this book. If you're a ministry or marketplace leader, do your organization a huge favor: equip your administrative teams, and position your organization for increased success by placing a copy of this book in the hands of all your admins; they will appreciate you for it. Who knows, such a gesture may even score you some much needed morale-booster points. If you're concerned about the budget, then just require them to go out and get this book, and perhaps even consider taking the entire admin team through a large or small group-reading intensive. You get the point, don't you?

Friend, in the pages that follow, an incredible and exciting journey awaits you. Now get cozy, grab that latte or whatever your thing is, and dive into to *The Super Kingdom Admin*!

Philip Anthony Mitchell

Introduction

In the fall of 2014, I was having a conversation with one of my brothers in Christ. He is a dynamic visionary who had started a church the year before. He had the foresight to assign administrators to every ministry in church; however, he was having some challenges. After a lengthy discussion, he asked me if I would consider coming and speaking to his Volunteer team.

I was surprised at the request but I was excited to fulfill it. I agreed, and in November 2014, on a cold Saturday, the weekend before Thanksgiving, I walked into a room of about 20 people (I was expecting five or six, 10 at the most).

That was the weekend on which "Super Kingdom Admin" was born. This book is an attempt to capture the experience and informational exchange which occurred on that day.

Since that day, I have presented this content to many other church administrative and support teams, and now I want to share it with you.

This book contains seven components that I firmly believe will forever change how you view your role and your ability to execute it.

These seven components are based on 20 overall years of ministry that I have spent in serving in the kingdom in various capacities: volunteer, ministry leader, contractor, part-time and full-time employee.

I am sure that you have heard of someone who received a job for which he or she was not qualified, but the Lord worked it out and the person got it anyway. Well, in my case of serving as an Executive Administrator, my story is a little like that. Actually, it is a lot like that. I have been a member of my present church for almost 10 years. During this time, I have served in a number of roles, but the one that actually qualifies me to write this book I never applied for. I was selected for it and accepted the call.

Almost five years later, I was approached about assuming the role of Executive Assistant to Senior Pastor, I was shocked and excited at the same time. I was shocked because at the time, I was a separated, single mother with four children (one in high school and the others in elementary). I was so honored not only by the request, but at my Pastor's faith in me to do the job, along with all of the other responsibilities I had at the time. I was excited because I knew that God had to be up to something because I had worked in an office before, but I was not formally trained in Administration. My bachelors' degree is in English, with a concentration in Mass Communications. I had been trained in layout design, copyediting, Public Relations, English, Journalism, Television/Audio Production. I had been using those skills for years, but an Executive Assistant; however, I was not sure of exactly all of what people working in this area did.

But, I had spent enough time around the two individuals who had the position before me to have a general idea. So I hit the ground running. I learned as much as I could about what my leader needed, liked and didn't like right away. The rest I will share with you on the pages you are about to read.

The kingdom administrator is a very unique role. It is not about just being a secretary, scheduler, or personal assistant who constantly runs errands. A kingdom administrator is someone who continually develops the skills needed to help the pastors and church leaders that he or she serves to be the very best they can be. A kingdom administrator understands that he or she is there to make the leaders' lives better (not worse) and to ease the weight of the load the leaders carry. It is not an easy job. Yet it is absolutely worth the sacrifice for the right leader in the right season.

The role is not only about performing duties and completing daily activities. It is also about having been called to serve while fulfilling duties and completing tasks.

Serving in this capacity has taught me valuable lessons about the functionality of an administrator and how to unlock the super powers of this extremely unique and highly important position.

I want to give you seven principles that you need to know and adhere to in order to unleash your super powers and become a "Super Kingdom Admin."

Let's go!

Chapter 1: Knowledge Component #1

Know Thyself

When I was growing up there was a group named *De La Soul* who popularized a song called "Me, Myself and I." The sentiment of that song is the first concept you will have to know in order to reach your kingdom capacity. You are going to have to know you better than you have ever known you before. At the end of the day, the things you don't know can hurt you when it comes to you. Nobody should know you better than you know yourself.

We live in an interesting time where people constantly are putting out the deepest, most intimate details about themselves on social media for the world to see. Then people obtain that information and have more information about those individuals than they should. That becomes an issue. Everyone does not need to know everything about you, your life, and your struggles.

There is one person however, who does need to have knowledge of all of that—the good, the bad and the ugly—that is you. You have to get to not only know you, you have to be committed to fixing what needs to be fixed and loving the "real" you. You will never survive working in the kingdom in any capacity if you are always living behind a mask. At some point, the mask will crack or break. If you have been promoted to the front lines of the battle, you can become severely wounded or worse, slaughtered, if you are trying to reassemble your mask in the heat of the battle. You have to resolve your issues before you show up to serve on the kingdom battle field.

Here are some things that you need to know about yourself if you are to become effective in being a "Super Kingdom Admin:"

A. You need to know your strengths.

If you are going to serve effectively, you must know your strengths. You must know what things you do well. There are different levels of strengths. You can do something well on a "beginner" level, which means that you can do it, but you may just be learning it. You can do something "proficiently," which means you do a good job at it. You know all the "nuts and bolts" of the mechanism and it works but that is it. Last, you have a skill set allows which you to feel as if you are an "expert" and are the top of the class in this subject matter.

List three of your strengths in the space below:

_____

_____

_____

B. You need to know your weaknesses.

Knowing your weaknesses is almost more critical than knowing your strengths. Nothing will mess you up more than thinking that you are better in an area than you really are. I will give you a quick example.

I told you earlier that I am the mother of four children. Well, at the time of this writing, I actually also have two stepchildren, as well as a son-in-law and a grandson. So I will reference them a great deal since they are an endless source of relevant material. Just wanted to let you know up front, so consider this fair warning.

Ok, so one of the things about having multiple children is that they are perfect examples of individuals who have the same DNA and live in the same environment, but they have different strengths and weaknesses. One example in my house is swimming. If you asked my three youngest daughters if they could all swim a few years ago, they would have all responded, "yes." But the truth is, one of them swims really well, and the other two just okay. Two of the girls I would categorize as "beginners" and one as proficient. None of them were truly advanced or expert swimmers, but they did not really know or accept that reality. So when we would take them swimming, we had to watch them because we knew that swimming for two of them was a weakness where they believed that they had strength.

This faulty thinking could have been extremely dangerous for them and if not closely monitored could have increased the possibility of their drowning if we had not kept them out of the 9-feet section of the pool. Similarly, you, too, can drown or die (physically, emotionally, mentally or spiritually) in the kingdom if you are not clearly aware of your weaknesses.

If you have struggled with addiction, you may not want to be involved in a Recovery project at your ministry until you have been delivered and set free for a while. The administrators serve a vitally important role in the ministry. If the enemy can distract and defeat those of us who provide organization and structure to the ministry, then he can paralyze and ultimately destroy that ministry, church, leader or pastor. Knowing your weaknesses, both personal and professional, is imperative.

List three of your weaknesses in the spaces provided below:

_____

_____

_____

C. You need to know your desires.

It is so super important for you to know your desires. You need to know what you really want. Knowing your desires will help you know how to approach your role in the ministry. There are a few types of ministry personnel. We will discuss in greater detail later in the book. For now we talk about: seasonal administrative workers and the type of administrators we refer to "lifers." Lifers have committed to working in this designated area of ministry until the Lord calls him or her home to glory. Your desires will often dictate which one of those categories you fall into.

Your desires will further help you know if you are called into volunteer service or if you are called to render full-time ministry service. There is a huge difference, and often, the sacrifice is tremendous. If you are someone who desires to make a great deal of money, working full-time in the kingdom may not be a good financial fit for you. In most instances, churches and ministries are non-profit organizations with smaller budgets and smaller salaries in comparison with similar organizations in the secular world. You have to make sure that you are okay with that reality, or whether you want to be a part of a larger church organization that can give you the salary you are seeking.

Last, you need to know what your "perfect world" looks like. In "your perfect world…" fill in the blank with what those items are. That will also help you determine if this is something that you will be doing seasonally or for life. There are people who start serving and realize that the kingdom requires a sacrifice that they have decided that they are not willing to make. It is much better to know that before you get into it. Working in the kingdom is not something that should be taken lightly. Your desires will help you properly weigh and calculate the costs to help you come to all the conclusions necessary for you to serve well and in a "clear-eyed manner."

Take a minute to write out your desires.

(What you want now, what you want in the future, what your "perfect world" looks like:)

_____

_____

_____

D. You need to know your destination.

Many times, people begin serving in church after a rough season. Some people go through a great deal of pain and anguish before committing to the Lord or returning to Him. It is very easy to mistake your gratitude of what the ministry has done for you as a "permanent full-time ministry call" when that may or may not be the case. We have all been given a mandate to call and to reach the lost and tell them about the Gospel of Jesus Christ. We are not all, however, called to serve in full-time ministry. Often, your destination is an indicator of your call. If your destiny is to be a doctor, then it is highly likely that you may have been called to work in Missions, or serve on Health or Medical team at church. However, your destination makes it highly likely that you are called to serve full time.

Sometimes, you can think you have your destination all figured out, and the Lord will completely re-route your plans. That really is my story. Every single time I came up with a new plan, something else I thought I was destined to do, none of those "destination" doors would open for me. Our pastor tells people, "Often, when you are truly called to ministry, no other doors will open for you. Sometimes, you end up realizing that it is God because He shuts all the other doors."

I have learned that you have seasonal destinations and permanent destinations. I will give you an example: There are some places to which I fly more often than others. My preference is always a non-stop flight. There are some cities to which I fly that non-stops are not an option. In those cases, I must have a connecting flight. My connecting flight is not my final destination. It is a place where I have to go to catch the next flight that will take me to my final destination. So take me, for example, the Lord has called me to do ministry in the marketplace with pastors and leaders; to work with women and single moms; and to spread the message of faith-packaged in a deliverance-style ministry. Yet, the Lord made my connecting flight an administrative and support-staff role. The time I have spent and am spending on this first leg of the flight is giving me everything I need for my destination. Think about it. On the first leg of the flight you fly down with one captain and crew. Once that plane lands, you connect and board with an entirely new captain and crew. You would never have gotten to your final destination without that plane change. Now, rarely, you have a plane stop, but not a plane change. In that instance, you may change seats on that plane, but you have the same the crew and captain. In the same way, you may have already arrived at the place that is going to give you everything you need for your final "called" destination, and you just have to wait for your seat to change. But you will not know what plane to get on if you don't know where your destination is.

No matter what you have to do: turn your plate down (and fast), talk to a mentor, pray with a friend, write a 5-year plan with your spouse/significant other, but do whatever you have to do to know where you are going. Nothing will impact your serving like knowing your destination.

What is your destination? At what point are you in your journey? If you are not sure, list a person or persons who can help you work out your destination details.

_____

_____

_____

_____

_____

E. You need to know your priorities.

1. Commitment

You must make commitment a priority. If you say you are going to do it, then you must do it. If the plan has to change for any reason, let the appropriate person(s) know right away. This courtesy shows your loyalty to your leader and to his or her vision. Loyalty is non-negotiable. If you can master this rare commodity, you will always be successful in life and in the kingdom. Indeed, loyalty is a precious Kingdom commodity that has become increasingly hard to find.

2. Communication

Communication is key. It is still an essential element, both professionally and personally. Emails are important. Letters are important. Calls are important. The critical key to communication in this day and time is knowing which method of communication is appropriate for each given occasion or task.

In the kingdom, it is even more important. Some things are just not "texting" appropriate. There are things that require a phone call, while other situations may call for a personal touch—such as a hand-written note or letter. We cannot let modern technology rob of us of the intimacy achieved through actual interaction.

The uppermost reason that I started texting on a phone is that I have a sister that is two years younger than I and there was a point in our lives where that means was the only way I could get in contact with her. After a time, my mother also started texting for that same reason. If we called my sister, our calls were always going to voicemail. Now dealing with embracing new forms of technology is actually nothing new.

I was blessed enough to be raised around several generations of my family. I knew both my maternal and paternal great-grandmothers as well as my maternal and paternal grandmothers and grandfathers.

My great-grandmothers were frustrated by the telephone. They felt as if people did not visit as they should because they could just call. My being young and never remembering a time without a telephone translates to this didn't really not making a lot of sense to me. Nevertheless, my grandmothers would always be fussing about calling people and finding the lines busy. (This was before "call waiting"). Then my dad would fuss about people's "not answering the beep" once "call waiting" came out. Then I remember my mom's fussing about one of her siblings who always seemed to have their answering machine on and that she always had to leave a message.

So the "communication war" continues to wage on. Now my parents get upset when our children bring their phones to the dinner table, and I am sure that it will continue. My point is that in the kingdom, we have to use technology for good and not for evil.

Take social media; we have to be careful that our social media accounts don't present a lukewarm representation of our Christian character. I especially tell young believers that it is crucial for them not to start their day with scriptures on their page and end it with #SquadGoals of themselves with their friends wearing very few clothes and participating in questionable activities. We have to communicate and illustrate that we are the "light and salt of the earth". We must be careful not to portray anything that is in direct opposition to that message. Communication in the kingdom and especially as an administrator is critical, crucial, and key.

3. Continuing Education

No matter how much you know, you can always learn more. You must keep learning. I have been blessed to attend C.E.A.S.E. conferences and workshops hosted by Beverly Robinson (the organization's co-founder and the executive assistant for Bishop TD Jakes). At the last conference I was able to attend, presenter Vickie Sokol Evans from Redcape said that over 75 percent of the suggestions that Microsoft receives to make the product better already exist within the software. That means there are a lot of people who think they know Microsoft better than they really do! We must all make a commitment to becoming lifelong learners because there is always more to learn.

4. Confidence.

If you are going to excel in the kingdom, you must have confidence. As I stated earlier, a lot of people get to the kingdom in a vehicle of pain, rejection, hurt and/or abandonment. The thing about rejection is that the pain of that situation can rob you of the God-given confidence that was given to you as a daughter or son of the Most-High God. Whatever you do, you cannot throw away your confidence.

Hebrews 10:35 reminds us:

So do not throw away your confidence; it will be richly rewarded.

There are a couple of things that I suggest you do so that your confidence levels don't drop.

A. Dress for where you are going and not where you have been, and keep the "Public you" together …

When my ex-husband and I separated, I decided then and there that I refused to look like what I was going through. My leaders always emphasized "image importance" to the leadership and staff. I embraced those teachings. I quickly concluded that I was going to get my image together, but I wanted it to be real. I realized that in order to walk into a room regally, I was going to have to look the part on the outside *and feel it on the inside*. I took time to heal, I journaled, and I cried—privately. Publically, however, I created a hair regiment that would allow me to have my hair together at all times. I started watching make-up tutorials to improve my application techniques. I started replacing outdated clothes in my closet that didn't fit by giving away the old ones and by using lay-away to purchase new ones. Now I have started assisting other women through fashion tips with a social media page called "Kingdom Couture." I truly believe that embracing your "queendom" is a part of your kingdom super powers!

B. Fully embrace "who you are in Him"

You are royalty. You are a "King's kid." You are a chosen generation, and you have indeed been chosen for a time such as this. Walk in your "kingdom nobility." Keep your head up, and surround yourself with confident people. Now there is a difference between proud, arrogant people and confident people. Confident people are good, solid individuals who are passionate about their purpose and are determined to pursue it. They are not jealous or envious, and they can cheer you on while you run in your lane, and you can cheer them while they run in their lane. They see you as their kingdom siblings and not life competitors.

5. Consistency

My leader has taught me that: "Consistency is a sign of competency." He uses the example that he knows someone can cut hair well when he or she cuts hair well all the time. If sometimes the hair is faded well and sometimes it is all jacked up, that person is not competent in the skill because he or she doesn't consistently perform it well. In the same way, you must get to a point that you consistently excel at the tasks that you perform. It is absolutely "mission essential" that you prioritize consistency.

Your Priorities:

Are there any of the 5 Priorities that you need to work on more than others? List the ones you think that you do well. Then list the ones you need to improve upon.

_____

_____

_____

_____

_____

_____

_____

_____

_____

_____

Prayer for You:

Lord, I am believing that every person who reads this section will begin to know himself or herself in a way that he or she had not previously known. I pray that You will give each of them the strength to admit his or her weaknesses, improve his or her strengths, align his or her desires with Your will and arrive at the destination that you pre-ordained for his or her before the foundation of the earth.

I pray that you will renew and restore confidence in each reader. I pray that you will birth a desire in him or her for continuing education that will equip him or her to grow in strength and wisdom. I pray that you will give him or her grace to become empowered for the journey ahead in Your Mighty Name, I pray. Amen.

Chapter 2: Knowledge Component #2

Know God For Yourself

"It's not my mother or my father, Lord, but it is me standing in the need of prayer!"—African-American Hymn "Standing in the Need of Prayer"

I am not sure if you have ever had someone in your life who you knew was praying for you. It may be, or have been, a mother, grandmother, father, sister, or brother. But if you have ever had someone like that in your life, then you know that that special someone is a blessing. Unfortunately, the longer you live on this side of glory, as long as you are breathing, you will learn something very important: there is nothing like knowing God for yourself.

You will discover that the prayers of the righteous are powerful, but there will come a point where you will have to know Him for yourself. That is critical knowledge when you are serving in the kingdom because you have enlisted in God's army. Not only are you serving in the army, but you are on the front line. There is absolutely no way you will survive without Him! Since that is the case, nothing is more important than your relationship with Him.

So let's take a minute to have a heart-to-heart by asking these questions:

- Do you know Him? Do you know him <u>for real</u>?
- Is He <u>really</u> Lord of your life?
- Do you have a healthy fear of the Lord and His commandments?

Proverbs 9:10 (TLB) reads:

For the reverence and fear of God are basic to all wisdom. Knowing God results in every other kind of understanding.

A healthy fear of the Lord helps you in every area of your life. It helps you live the best possible life you can and makes eternal life guaranteed for you. Your knowing God and maintaining a healthy fear of his laws is not only a matter of heaven and hell; it is also the difference between receiving blessings or curses.

In Isaiah 1:18-20 (NIV) it says:

18 "Come now, let us settle the matter," says the Lord. "Though your sins are like scarlet, they shall be as white as snow; though they are red as crimson, they shall be like wool. 19 If you are willing and obedient, you will eat the good things of the land; 20 but if you resist and rebel, you will be devoured by the sword." For the mouth of the Lord has spoken.

The interesting thing about this verse is that even though we are all born into sin and shaped in iniquity there is an antidote for living under curses. That antidote is obedience. Obedience is virtually impossible without a relationship with our Father in Heaven. He gives us the revelation to see its importance and the strength to commit to it. God loves us so much that He gave us free will. We always have a choice.

We can see the choice clearly in Deuteronomy 30:15-16 (NIV):

15 See, I set before you today life and prosperity, death and destruction. 16 For I command you today to love the Lord your God, to walk in obedience to him, and to keep his commands, decrees and laws; then you will live and increase, and the Lord your God will bless you in the land you are entering to possess.

Choosing God will allow you to live your best life yet and shield you from death and destruction.

So after you chose Him, you must commit to knowing Him. If you already have a serious, "no-joke" relationship with the Lord, I want to encourage you to go deeper. The Word promises that when you seek Him with your whole heart, you will find Him.

There are several reasons your relationship with God is so important, especially while you are serving the men, women, and people of God.

1- You have a spiritual role to play with your leader.
Exodus 17:8-13 reads:

8 The Amalekites came and attacked the Israelites at Rephidim. 9 Moses said to Joshua, "Choose some of our men and go out to fight the Amalekites. Tomorrow I will stand on top of the hill with the staff of God in my hands."

10 So Joshua fought the Amalekites as Moses had ordered, and Moses, Aaron and Hur went to the top of the hill. 11 As long as Moses held up his hands, the Israelites were winning, but whenever he lowered his hands, the Amalekites were winning. 12 When Moses' hands grew tired, the men with him took a stone and put it under him, and he sat on it. Aaron and Hur held his hands up—one on one side, one on the other—so that his hands remained steady till sunset. 13 So Joshua overcame the Amalekite army with the sword.

While Joshua and the men were fighting, Moses held up his staff in his hands. As long as Moses' hands were up, Joshua and their men were winning. When Moses' hands got tired and his hands lowered their enemies began to defeat them. So Aaron and Hur held up Moses' hands, one under the other, so that his hands remained steady until the battle was won.

You have to be ready to "hold up" the arms of your leader. You <u>have to be ready</u>. You <u>have to be strong</u>. You <u>have to be willing</u>. If you are not spiritually strong, you will never be equipped to help your leader win the war. And surely, the kingdom of God is at war. We have an enemy who desires to sift us all as wheat. If we are going to advance and declare victory for God in the time and culture in which we live, it is going to require your having a super, strong relationship with God. You are going to have to know Him and develop your relationship with Him more and more, day after day.

Take a moment and consider: is there any sin in your life? If so, make it a point to deliberately spend time with God daily. This is an excellent way to drive the enemy out.

2- You have a spiritual role to play with your team.

Aaron and Hur helped their team achieve success. The role that they played in assisting Moses caused their entire team to score a victory.

When you are not in right relationship with God and when you make a decision to live beneath God's standards, you put place your entire team in jeopardy.

In Joshua chapters 6 and 7, we see that Achan's transgression of taking a robe, two hundred shekels of silver, and a bar of gold weighing fifty shekels had two devastating effects.

TWO EFFECTS OF ACHAN'S SIN:

1- HIS ACTIONS RESULTED IN HIS TEAM'S DEFEAT.
Up until this point, Joshua's team had been undefeated. Achan messes up. He steals from the camp and the very next battle his people fight, they lose. All of this occurs because of Achan's disobedience.

2- HIS ACTIONS COST HIM & HIS FAMILY THEIR LIVES
The punishment for Achan's sin was death. He was not the only one to be killed: his entire family also suffered his same fate.

Your relationship with God is extremely important. When you walk with God and you serve His people, you must continually decide to keep serving Him and obeying His commandments. Your inability to do this could cost your leader, your team, your family and yourself. Let's discuss another way your spiritual life can affect your family.

The Spiritual Role You Play for Your Family

Joshua 2:8-13

> *8 Before the spies lay down for the night, she went up on the roof 9 and said to them, "I know that the Lord has given you this land and that a great fear of you has fallen on us, so that all who live in this country are melting in fear because of you. 10 We have heard how the Lord dried up the water of the Red Sea for you when you came out of Egypt, and what you did to Sihon and Og, the two kings of the Amorites east of the Jordan, whom you completely destroyed. 11 When we heard of it, our hearts melted in fear and everyone's courage failed because of you, for the Lord your God is God in heaven above and on the earth below. 12 "Now then, please swear to me by the Lord that*

you will show kindness to my family, because I have shown
kindness to you. Give me a sure sign 13 that you will spare the
lives of my father and mother, my brothers and sisters, and all
who belong to them—and that you will save us from death."

When the spies went into the land, they needed a place to hide.
Rahab got them out of harm's way, and in exchange, saved her entire
family. Rahab actions prove that your spiritual decisions can pro-
duce a positive outcome for your immediate family and multiple
generations to come.

(Know therefore that the Lord your God is God; he is the faith-
ful God, keeping his covenant of love to a thousand generations
of those who love him and keep his commandments. Deuteron-
omy 7:9 NIV)

Rahab's decision also resulted in her family's becoming a part of
the bloodline of the Messiah! In the first chapter of Matthew we see
that Rahab married Salmon of the tribe of Judah and was the mother
of Boaz. You can read the genealogy details in the first chapter of the
book of Matthew. Rahab's decision charted the destiny for her family,
and you have that same power, too.

Just as Rahab's life was changed forever by that one decision,
you are capable of crafting a new destiny for your family as well. It
all starts with pursuing a deeper relationship with God. Your relationship with your Heavenly Father is important because of the
benefits it produces for you and all those who are connected to
you. God is faithful when we are not faithful, but He is even *more*
faithful to the faithful.

So now you know that you are completely aware of how important knowing God is, you may wonder how you can get to know Him
or how you can know Him" better"?

The first step in getting to know God is making a decision to do it. After making the decision, you must commit to maintaining a very specific and strategic lifestyle.

Your Commitment requires a lifestyle of prayer, praise, meditating on the Word, and positive affirmations.

This lifestyle requires that:

1. You pray to God.
Praying to God just means you talk to Him. You are in consistent communication with the Lord. Sometimes this may mean kneeling beside your bed. At other times, it may mean that you are reflecting on scriptures and quietly meditating in your car, and at other times it may mean praying in a prayer language *(if you have been filled/or believe in infilling)*. Prayer means different things to different people, but one thing is the same: prayer connects you to God and allows you to know Him better. He will reveal things to you during this time, and those revelations will help you in every area of your life.

2. You praise and worship God.
Singing songs to the Lord helps you to get into His presence. Melodies and hymns can help lift heaviness, depression, anxiety and fear from you. Outward displays of thanksgiving and expressions of gratitude can be demonstrated by praising the Lord in a church service. If you are a Pentecostal or charismatic believer, you may display this association by shouting and dancing with great motion and expression. If not, your praise and worship may be more serene by the gesture of bowing, lying prostrate and calling on His Name. Gospel, Christian, and inspirational songs all contribute to welcoming the presence of God into the atmosphere. Any environment can be changed once praise and worship begin. It is important to learn to participate in praise and worship in other places besides church. When you work in

the kingdom, whether as a paid-staff member or as a member of the volunteer support staff, there are times where you may miss service. You cannot afford to only get into the presence of the Lord on service days and nights. You must keep yourself drenched in His presence. I am not saying that you should never listen to secular music, but you should definitely be listening to more things that edify your spirit than any other type of music.

3. You meditate on the Word on God.

You must take some time to learn God's Word and meditate on it day and night. It is impossible for you to know God and keep His commandments if you don't know what those commandments say. Knowing the Word will help you in the busy ministry seasons when you cannot always be in an entire service. In addition to reading the bible on your own, you can sign up for bible devotions to come to you daily in your email, and you can also listen to sermons and messages from other leaders who feed your soul. If your church has an online archive where you can go back and watch the messages you missed, then you should take advantage of that as well. You must keep your soul fed while you are helping the shepherds feed and minister to the sheep.

4.You must speak life and not death. You surround yourself with people who speak life and not death.

One of the most important aspects of your relationship with God is what you say. You will have what you say; there is no question about that. At the end of this section, I will show you how to create an affirmation for your life. Sometimes when you have been through challenges and have been or are surrounded by negativity, an affirmation is something that can be repeated over and over until you have built your faith back up and driven negative forces away from you. While you are implementing this positive affirmation, it is key that you also stop hanging around people who bring negativity back into your atmosphere.

If you are really going to know God, you must be determined to surround yourself with people who speak life and not death. If you are going to work in the kingdom and be successful, you are going to have to hang out with mostly "kingdom kids." If you are going to truly unleash your super kingdom admin powers you must learn to be super selective and absolutely intentional about your inner circle and the company you keep. The reason your circle is so important is that because when you want to talk badly enough the wrong circle will do. You cannot afford to have the "wrong" people around you. Now, as believers, we are admonished to be "in" the world and not "of" it. This means that we cannot speak only to Christians and be around only Christians. What it does mean is that the closest people to you should be committed to the same lifestyle you are trying to live. If those people aren't saved, then you should be pulling them closer to salvation than they are capable of pulling you toward sin. If you find yourself slipping away from the clutches of your faith after being around certain individuals, you may have to limit the time you are around them.

For the last decade, I have been serving and submitted to a leader who does an amazing job describing the types of relationships you need in order to be successful in the kingdom.

Pastor Andy Thompson describes them as "3 Levels of Accountability":

1. **Up Relationships:** These are relationships in which you are looking up to someone who can mentor you. These are people who you look to for advice and counsel. During one of the Super Kingdom Admin sessions I had a revelation about the "Up Relationships" that I think will help as it helped the admins in the

workshop that day. The "Up Relationships" are best described as like a traffic or stoplight:

A. RED LIGHT

Up Relationships help you know when it is time to STOP. Up Relationships help you see when you are going in the wrong direction, and you just need to stop. You may be going too fast. There may be something coming that they have the wisdom and experience to see that you cannot see. No matter what the reason is, when a mentor, pastor, leader or parent (that you trust and has no ulterior motives) tells you to stop, then you need to stop.

B. YELLOW LIGHT

Up Relationships help you know when it is time to slow down. These are people in your life who give you warnings and sound the alarm on decisions that may need some thought or a little more time. Often, God will send them at just the right time to help you determine the feasibility of your actions and the timing of them as well.

C. GREEN LIGHT

Up Relationships help you know when it is time to go! Sometimes you need someone in your life on the sidelines just cheering you on! Sometimes you need someone to tell you it is time to do it. Sometimes you need someone to ask you, "What are you waiting for?" Sometimes you need someone to remind you, "There is no time like the present." Sometimes you need someone to remind you that "you" will not be young forever or that even though "you" may be old, it's never too late to pursue something that God pre-destined for you to achieve before the foundation of the Earth! Sometimes you just need a push, a shove, or a loving speech (often very long) to get you up and going.

If you have Up Relationships value them. If you don't have any, you need to be prayerfully seeking them.

2. **Across Relationships:** My leader also taught me that these ("Across" relationships) are your most honest relationships. You are more likely to tell "across" comrades the truth. Sometimes in "Up Relationships," you are trying to act as if you have it more together than you really do. "Across" relationships are peer relationships. These are your friends on the same level as you. You are often in similar stations of life. Again, if you don't have any friends who are trying to be saved and are on a path to success as you, then you need to carefully re-evaluate those friendships. Many people in my family (including my parents and sister) attended the HBCU—NC Central University. Our mascot is the Eagle. My dad used to tell me that one of the slogans that was said about our alma mater was, "The eagle is no common barnyard foul." Well, I love that, because it was always a reminder to me that chickens were limited to the ground, but Eagles were built to soar. So no matter how discouraged I became, I was constantly reminded that I belonged in the air, soaring with the Eagles and that I would never remain grounded in the barnyard with the chickens. I want to make you all honorary Eagles today. You need to find the other Eagles in your life and all soar together.

3. **Down Relationships:** You need people in your life who are looking up to you. You need mentees, spiritual sons, daughters, nieces and nephews who can look to you for advice. They need to be able to call upon you for wisdom. When you have people

looking up to you, there are just some things that you are more likely not to do. You are less likely to do something that those people would be ashamed of—anything that would disqualify you from leadership in their eyes. It helps you maintain your relationship to God because you are also seeking Him on their behalf. You are praying for someone other than yourself. If you have experienced loss, tragedy or hurt, then take some time and allow God to heal you before you attempt to pour into someone else. It may take seasons of you allowing God to restore you and build you up before you have enough stored within you to pour out. After you are healed and renewed, be sure that you don't wait too long to find someone to pour into. That individual needs it, and so do you!

If you are going to know God on a deeper level, following are just a few of the things that you should consider in order to shift your relationship with Him and know Him in ways you never could have imagined!

Know-God-Reflection Time

Do you have any areas in your life that you are struggling with, that make it difficult to totally surrender your life, will, soul, mind and body to the Lord? If "yes," list them here. Commit these areas to prayer and share them with a friend or leader you trust. If this does not apply to you, list the names of some individuals who are on your team, whom you feel may be experiencing difficulty in this area, and commit to praying for them.

_____

_____

_____

_____

_____

_____

_____

What are some ways you would like to be more of a blessing to your leader after seeing the spiritual role you play?

_____

_____

_____

_____

_____

Do you feel like as though you are the best team member you can be (through your life and actions)? *If no, list ways you can become better. If "yes," list the names of team members you would like to see make progress in this area.*

_____

_____

_____

_____

What are some ways you can play a bigger role in helping your family members find their purpose and destiny in God?

_____

_____

_____

_____

_____

_____

_____

In this chapter, we discussed the importance of developing a lifestyle that included: *prayer, praise, worship, meditating on the Word, affirmations and positive people.*

What are some times and days of the week you could commit to dedicating time with the Lord?

_____

_____

_____

_____

_____

_____

_____

List some of your favorite Christian/Gospel artists on the lines below. Then research some new artists, and list them.

Now take some time to purchase their music and create playlists or get CDs to listen to the music "on the go." Make it a point to saturate your atmosphere with these praise and worship songs on a daily/weekly basis.

_____

_____

_____

_____

_____

NEW ARTISTS:

_____

_____

_____

_____

List 2 Scriptures that always give you peace and hope.

_____

_____

_____

_____

List 1 Biblical Character who always encourages you and where his or her story is found in the Bible:

_____

_____

_____

For the next 30-90 days, I would like to encourage you to read Psalms and Proverbs. Select five Scriptures to memorize, and list the verses below (if you run out of room, you can always get a journal that you use only for writing scriptures in). The verses you select here and for your Scripture Journal will be tremendously helpful in implementing the Word into your life and daily routine.

_____

_____

_____

_____

_____

Create an Affirmation for your life.
Here is an example:

I am delivered from sin.
God is the ruler of my life.
I can do all things through Him.
He strengthens me.
I have never seen the righteous forsaken, nor his seed begging for bread;

Therefore, I know that He will never forsake me or my seed.

Even on my darkest days, I know that God is Jireh Provider.

Even in times of sickness, I know that God is Jireh Rophe.

Even in times of trouble, I know that God is Jehovah Nissi (my banner) and that

He always fights for me.

As a matter of fact, no weapon that forms against me can prosper because the battle is not mine anyway. It is the Lord's!

So I can go ahead and shout because Victory is Mine!

I will see the goodness of the Lord in the Land of the Living, and

The number of my days He will fulfill.

I will wait on the Lord and be of good courage because the good work my God began in me, He will be faithful to complete it.

Amen.

Your affirmation should deal with the things that you are facing. Your affirmation should contain scripture to back it up. Your affirmation should be a reminder to you of the victory, while encouraging you in difficult times. You should memorize it and make it a part of your meditation time. This doesn't have to be the last or only one you do. It should be the first one. If the one above applies to you, start with it, and add or subtract the parts that don't apply or parts that you would like to change. Positive affirmations can change your life. I encourage you to create one today. You can practice on scraps of paper, and write the final version of yours here. (Feel free to also type it up and post it other places in your bathroom, home, or office).

_____

_____

_____

The last assignment in this section is about your inner circle. You need up, across, and down relationships to keep you anchored. You don't need many, just a "select" few.

If you have 1-3 people in each category, you are doing fairly well. (*I suggest more than 1 across relationship because if you have only one and he or she is in a busy season, you can find yourself lacking in this category really quickly.*)

List your UP RELATIONSHIPS:

1.

2.

3.

List your ACROSS RELATIONSHIPS

1.

2.

3.

List your DOWN RELATIONSHIPS

1.

2.

3.

Prayer for you:

Lord, I pray as we all endeavor to know you better that you would begin to walk with us and allow us to feel Your presence as never before. You said that we would find you when we seek after you with our whole hearts. We are seeking you now, completely, withholding anything. We ask you to fill every crevice of our hearts with Your Love and Peace. We desire to know You as we never have so that we can be more and do more in your Kingdom, for your servants and your people. We are empty vessels coming to be filled by You so that we can forever pour out your goodness, grace and mercy on others. Please be with us, guide us, and we will be so careful to give You the honor, glory and the praise for everything You do. In Jesus' Name we pray! Amen.

Chapter 3: Knowledge Component #3

Know Your Leader

If you are going to activate your super admin powers, you must make a commitment to fulfilling the instructions in this chapter. There is no way you will adequately serve a man or woman of God that you do not take the time to get to know.

As I begin to travel and work with churches I am always amazed at the number of people who passionately serve leaders whom they often don't know very well at all. I do not mean "hang out" with the Senior Pastor and frequent his or her home. I am talking about individuals who serve leaders but do not know their "story."

I am challenging you to make this a top priority. If you already know your leader, make it your business to make sure that you assist your team leaders by sharing it with them, as well as, by sharing it with the new members who come into your organization. If you are serving in a ministry, church, or even an organization, and you do not know the Visionary's story, you need to know it. That is the first step of getting to know your leader and serving him or her well. So that is the first key I want to share with you:

A. Know His/Her Story

There are several pastors I will be mentioning numerous times. It is because their stories have helped to seriously shape how I <u>do</u> ministry, how I <u>see</u> ministry and the <u>help</u> I am able to give you right now. One of those pastors in Pastor Philip Mitchell, founder and senior pastor of Victory Church, Atlanta. When I presented "Super Kingdom Admin" at his church, this is one of the key points I gave to his team. I wanted to share with them a version of the story that their leaders may not have shared with them. It is always rewarding when a leader has someone who is close to him or her who can share the leader's story. Sometimes when men and women of integrity share the story, they play down the sacrifice because they are always sensitive about touching any of God's glory (and rightfully so). They want to make sure that the story's focus is on God and not on them. That is an honorable intent. However, the reason that you need to know the "story" and the intensity of it is that when you know what your Pastor or Leader has sacrificed for the vision, it is easier for you to sacrifice. It is easy to give to a ministry when you know that your leader has emptied out his or her savings account to start the organization/fellowship that is blessing you! It is easy to get up early on Sunday morning and be a part of a break-down and set-up team when you know that the furniture you are setting up with was purchased in faith. Often, when leaders start ministries, they "gamble" in the natural to do something that is a sure bet in the faith realm. Pastor Phil and his wife Lena are not the only ones! I know countless numbers of church planters who often possess a faith that is so audacious that it appears insane to everyone else! There are pastors who leave family, leave jobs, leave hometowns, and/or leave property all to start ministries for God. These men and women of God answer the call on their lives, and often, it costs them everything. When you understand their "story," what they gave up, what brought them to the place where they are today, such monumental courage should make it easier for you to follow them. It should make you want to follow them, and knowing your leader's/pastor's "story" should make you want to invite others to follow your leader as well.

If you are going to know your leader well, the next thing you need to know:

B. Know His/Her Heart

It is important for you to understand the "heart" of the leader you are serving. One of the most significant reasons you to need to know your leader's heart is that essentially, his or heart remains the same. There is a way that your leaders see ministry that is shaped by his or her own individual experiences, lessons, and values. While serving Pastor Andy Thompson, for example, I learned his heart was for people to receive relevant teaching in a balanced way. His heart's cry is that believers are able to live good days on Earth, not only in Heaven. Pastor Phil Mitchell has a heart for the lost. His church has a mantra based on His heart: "Until All Have Heard." The heart of a leader is important at all levels of ministry, not only at the Senior-Pastor or Lead-Pastor level. When my oldest daughter Chynah was growing up in youth ministry at our church, her youth pastor drilled into them that they had "one life" and that they needed to become as serious about living for God as early as possible. She is not perfect, but at the age of 20, she is an entrepreneur and married, and has borne her first child. She grabbed hold of that message that her youth pastor had shared with all of his heart. All of these pastors are changing lives and impacting the kingdom because of what God has specifically placed within their individual hearts. That youth pastor went on to become Founder/Senior Pastor of Nikao Church where he is still passionate about teaching and serving people. His vision slogan is "We is greater than me."

Each Pastor's heart affects his or her vision. It is important to know the heart of your leader before the vision because the vision changes, but the heart remains consistent throughout the leader's ministry. That assertion leads us right into our next key:

C. Know His/Her Vision

It is important to pay attention to a leader in every "season," because although his heart is consistent (as we stated above) the vision will vary. In one season, a Pastor's objectives may require a season of fasting and praying as a part of meeting the burden God has placed on his or her heart. The Vision always is a vehicle to accomplishing the "heart mission" of your leader. The vehicle changes over time, but it will always align with the burden for the people that God has placed upon the leader. In some seasons, the leader's vision may be financially focused. The Lord may lead him or her to see his congregants walk out the scriptures that tell us to be "lenders and not borrowers." Likewise, the leader may become severely concerned with the health of his members. Pastor Drew Ross wrote a book called <u>Overcome</u> about his weight-loss journey and was transparent with his members and community about his battle. He also encouraged them to walk out his plan for 90 days. Many of them committed to it and are seeing amazing results. No matter what the vision of your leader is at any given time, once you are in alignment with it and understand how it connects to his heart, it will be easier for you to help him accomplishment it.

Last, after you know your leader's "story," "heart" and vision, you must learn to recognize his or her voice.

D. Know His/Her Voice

John 10:3-5;11-18 (NIV) reads:

3 The gatekeeper opens the gate for him, and the sheep listen to his voice. He calls his own sheep by name and leads them out. 4 When he has brought out all his own, he goes ahead of them, and his sheep follow him because they know his voice. 5 But they will never follow a stranger; in fact, they will run away from him because they do not recognize a stranger's voice."

11 "I am the good shepherd. The good shepherd lays down his life for the sheep. 12 The hired hand is not the shepherd and does not own the sheep. So when he sees the wolf coming, he abandons the sheep and runs away. Then the wolf attacks the flock and scatters it. 13 The man runs away because he is a hired hand and cares nothing for the sheep. 14 "I am the good shepherd; I know my sheep and my sheep know me— 15 just as the Father knows me and I know the Father—and I lay down my life for the sheep. 16 I have other sheep that are not of this sheep pen. I must bring them also. They too will listen to my voice, and there shall be one flock and one shepherd. 17 The reason my Father loves me is that I lay down my life—only to take it up again. 18 No one takes it from me, but I lay it down of my own accord. I have authority to lay it down and authority to take it up again. This command I received from my Father."

As your church grows, your leader may designate others to relay information to the team. You must make sure that you know the voice of your leader. Nothing can sink a "church ship" faster than this one phrase: "Pastor said…"

You must know the voice of your shepherd, and another you must not follow. You should be respectful. You should not cause a scene, but you will have to find a way to verify the information, especially if it is something major that could have a negative impact on the leader, the team morale, or the members. As an administrator, you will be in a prime position to the leader better than a good many people. You must make sure you are Abigail when you need to be. Abigail was a woman in the bible who saved her entire household because she had to correct a life-threatening situation brought on by her husband Nabal against King David. Abigail's quick thinking and even quicker actions saved all of their lives. You don't want to make a habit of rebelling against other associate pastors or team leaders. However, you do want to make sure that the vision is accurately being communicated. There are times when you are often the eyes and ears of your pastor, and you have an obligation to make sure that he is aware if there is a possible miscommunication at play.

If you take the time to know your leader's "story," "heart," vision, and voice, you will serve him/her at a highly effective and impactful level. That will make a difference, not only in your local church, but for the kingdom at large.

Know Your Leader Reflection Time

Do you know your leader's story? If not, write down a time that you think you may be able to learn it from the leader or a team member who has been there longer than you. If you know the story, list a new team member who would benefit from hearing the story from you.

_____

_____

_____

_____

_____

What is the "heart" of your leader? What are the things that he or she is most passionate about? If you are not sure, ask your leader or a team member close to him/her or who has been there longer than you.

_____

_____

_____

_____

_____

_____

What is the current vision of your leader? What unique gifts, skills, and abilities do you possess that could assist in bringing that vision to fruition faster?

_____

_____

_____

_____

_____

Read the John 10 passage again. Reflect on times when you felt as if someone was communicating something that was not completely in alignment with your Pastor's voice. Were you correct/incorrect?

_____

Take some time to study John 10, and pray that God will increase your discernment in this area and your wisdom on how to navigate these situations when they arise. List any revelation God gives to you while reading this passage.

John 10 Study Notes:

_____

_____

_____

_____

_____

Prayer for You:

Lord, we thank you for the leaders you have placed in our lives. We desire to know them in a way that will allow us to serve them more sincerely, more excellently and with a more faithful precision that accelerates his/her kingdom assignments and brings them to pass with ease. We pray for healthy boundaries with our leaders and among our team. We tear down strongholds and pray against people who attempt to sow discord and division. We thank you in advance for removing anything from us that is not like you. We also thank you for removing any person from our team with impure motives. We pray against character assassins, controlling-witchcraft-Jezebel spirits, and we pray for team members who display the fruit of the spirit. Help us be all that we need to be for the men and women whom we serve. Allow us to lighten our leaders' loads while you continue to be a light unto their feet and a lamp unto their paths.

In Jesus' Name we pray.
Amen

Chapter 4: Knowledge Component #4

Know the Importance of Your Role

One of the most critical areas of kingdom administration is to know well and to fulfill your God-ordained role in the life of your leader to the best of your ability. Often the position "administrator/assistant" appears to be a glamorized and coveted one, but that is only because many individuals do not realize the true work and responsibility that go into it.

The ostensible glamor of the position quickly diminishes for anyone who truly finds himself or herself carrying out this job. The truth of the matter is that this position (and the kingdom in general) requires more than a little sacrifice. Honestly, you must make a sacrifice as an individual. However, I do not want to suggest that you should sacrifice your family, health or faith to do any job in the kingdom. Those types of sacrifice are not biblical. Therefore, it would be very unwise to jeopardize any of the aforementioned.

The first major revelation essential to grasp is that you have accepted this position to make your leader(s) lives better. Your job and individual job description will lay out the details of what your leaders need you to accomplish for them. These role requirements will help you carry out those tasks more effectively. The following represent five primary ways that you can achieve great success:

A. You need to anticipate his or her needs.

This anticipation is a fundamental component of knowing your role. The ability to give your leader something before he or she asks for it is invaluable. It represents one of the most powerful super admin powers. This ability is not something that happens overnight, but eventually it becomes second nature to a vigilant and perceptive admin. A way to remember importance of this role is to focus tirelessly on these three words: know, flow and go.

First, you must get to <u>know</u> your leader. Learn his or her preferences, and adjust to his or her temperament. Develop the ability to sense when he or she may be experiencing a challenge without his or her sharing it with you. Once you are around him or her long enough, you go from just <u>knowing</u> your leader to <u>flowing</u> with your leader.

Flowing with the leader means that you can adapt quickly to changes and that you can develop the ability to be flexible. Also, you have to be *flexible*. You aren't *strong* if you can't adjust. My leader frequently says: "True strength is seen in flexibility not in rigidity." This ability is best demonstrated during a natural storm. A tree that cannot bend will break. I have traveled to Florida a great deal in the last year. It rains quite frequently there, and when the wind begins to blow, often the palm tree fronds are almost touching the ground because the tree is leaning so far over. Although the tree looks thin and as though it should break, it doesn't. You can determine how strong the tree is because of the flexibility of the palm tree trunk. It adjusts back to normal when the storm is over. You must be able to be flexible in that way. The kingdom life will test you, your leader, and your church/ministry. You must be ready to flow, and last, you *go* with your leader.

You must stay ready to go and pre-plan items that he or she may need. Remaining ready to go, you become proactive and avoid procrastination. Procrastination is a ministry killer because there is always a new thing to do. If you are still working on the old assignment when the new assignment comes, you will always be behind. You have to move quickly, yet efficiently, to always be ready to *go* to the next assignment, place, or level!

B. You must develop excellent communication with your leader.

Many distracting and nettlesome issues can be avoided with proper communication. Communication with leaders can be tricky. Therefore, you must learn the best form of communication with your leaders. If you are communicating in a format that your leader(s) do not use, this difference can become an immediate issue. Some preferences are generation-related. If you serve an older leader (depending on his or her age), he or she may prefer a phone call as opposed to a text message or email, but not necessarily. The best bet is to be sure and only way to be sure is to ask. And even after you ask, you may have to check in periodically to be sure that the method preference has not changed.

Next, you also need to get a gauge on the frequency of communication your leader requires. Some leaders want to talk to you daily, others weekly, and some only when absolutely necessary. Some leaders like activity reports while others only want to know that you have gotten your work done. If you have a job description, the pertinent information may be found within it. If not, you should check with your leader, team leader, or Human Resources officer.

Also, be sure you are communicating immediately when plans change. Leaders are under a tremendous amount of pressure and depend on us to help relieve as much of it as possible. Developing and maintaining excellent communication practices with your leader is absolutely an admin super power which you by all means must put into practice.

This next way you make your leaders' lives better is to:

C. Become solution-oriented and not problem-focused.

Have you ever worked with someone who sees *everything* as a problem? If you have not, you are blessed! If you have, you know that those individuals can be a drag to be around. The negativity seems to ooze through his or her pores (figuratively speaking). Over time, team members treat the negative person very differently. Often team members intentionally shorten the interactions with this kind of person, or worse, avoid the negative individual altogether. Sounds pretty uncomfortable, doesn't it? Well, it becomes much worse in a leader/administrator position. The pressures that your leaders face daily are surreal. They must surround themselves with people who come to them with "the solution." I know that we just discussed communication and that you should communicate quickly when the plans change and trouble arises. However, I would like to suggest that you take a few quick to minutes and craft your delivery of the news you are about to share with your leader. For example, instead of saying:

"Pastor, the finance team did not approve my original request." Try this:

"Pastor, it looks as if we over shot the budget for the submitted project. Do you mind if we adjust the number of promo materials we order and eliminate the outdoor tents? If you are okay with that, I believe that the project will still be successful without putting a financial strain on the ministry."

In one scenario, you are presenting a problem; in the other, you are offering a solution. If you develop the ability to see the solutions and not the problems, you will find yourself becoming more successful in every area of your life.

Speaking of seeing the solution…a way to see the solution is to limit your "negativity intake." This one may or may not apply to you, but if it does you must:

D. Fall out of love with DRAMA

We have become a nation and a world absolutely obsessed with drama. It starts at an early age. For instance, almost everyone runs to the fight that breaks out on the playground. This continues into adulthood. For example, you end up on the road longer (often moving at a snail's pace) after a traffic accident because everyone is trying to get a glimpse of what happened. The drama-obsession doesn't end with everyday life. There are more reality TV shows on the air than ever. These shows would not be playing if no one was watching them. The ratings are "through the roof" because the viewers just can't get enough. Now, if reality shows are your thing, I am not trying to condemn you. I am just saying that you need to be mindful of your mounting unconscious negativity and drama intake. For some, it is an escape; for others, it becomes a mantra for how to live life. Such practices are not helpful to you or your leaders. You want to make sure that you are someone who exhibits a peaceful nature. This admonition is much easier said than done. It would be heavenly if you liked every one in ministry and everyone liked you, but unfortunately, your position alone can make people dislike you. When you serve the men and women of God closely, some people will envy that role. What they see on the outside is your proximity to the leader. Sometimes they associate proximity with influence, which may or may not be the case. In any instance, you have to develop intestinal fortitude pretty quickly. If you are someone who needs to be loved by everyone, however, you may need to serve in another area because often, unfortunately, receiving an all-encompassing love will rarely the case. In the same way, you must become an exceptional team player. I have found that I had to work extra hard to prove to the team that I don't think of myself "more highly than I should." It can be a tough balancing act because it can be difficult if you are the leader's messenger. It becomes really easy for you to become the "whipping boy." Next thing you know, people are taking out their frustrations on you (their displaced aggression) because they cannot tell the leader how they really feel—or at least not tell him or her without ramifications. At the end of the day, the more positive you keep your atmosphere and your environment, the more it will help you deal with the difficulties that come along with "people challenges" associated with your position.

Speaking of challenges, just know that:

E. You should do everything within your power not to make the same mistake repeatedly.

Your leader should not ask you for something twice without your having it, if it is within your capability. During my time as serving as an assistant one of the things that I learned quickly is that this role will test you. Sometimes a leader may test you. They may change up on you to see if you are on your toes. I don't want to make you paranoid, more often, the leaders change because they receive new information or insight. At one time, my leader drank only lemon-lime Gatorade. Later, he changed. He switched to drinking the frost ones with no dye. Then for two months, he didn't want any at all. Then all of a sudden, he needed them every week. So I began to stock them all the time. Even when a pastoral care committee was established for him, I still made sure we had extras. I never wanted him to ask me for one again and find that we not have the "latest preference of the day." Once you reach this level of capability, if you ever find yourself forgetting things that you normally remember or are no longer experiencing your usual productivity, one of three things may be occurring:

1. Your position is temporary or short-term, and it is winding up.

2. You may be suffering from burnout.

3. You may have been called to the position for a season, but your season could be drawing close to an end.

If you are in the first category, just know that the kingdom admin position is not for the faint of heart. It requires all of the attributes and qualifications of an administrator working in the secular world, but with the added component of being on the front line of God's army. Some individuals are called to work in this capacity only for a season of his or her life, especially if you have significant changes in your life that often can affect your ability to serve on a completely effective level. It is nothing to be ashamed of. You need to acknowledge the changes that are taking place and openly discuss them with your leader or Human Resources professional.

Next, if you are called to be what some refer to as a kingdom "lifer," then you have to be efficient at establishing times of rest and recognizing the Sabbath in some capacity for your life. If you don't, you will eventually burn out.

The ministry life is not a drive on the autobahn. When I lived in Germany as young a woman, I was fascinated by the concept of driving on a road with no speed limit. Well, my fascination quickly disappeared when I realized how fast cars really could go. This revelation can be compared to ministry life. It can be fascinating and feel really good to move at the speed of the light all the time, but the truth is that you cannot endure at that pace. You need to maneuver through your ministry life by figuratively taking the scenic route occasionally. After you have completed all the "mission essential" tasks, it is okay to take a break. Schedule your vacation, and when you go away, try your best to completely unplug. If all you do is work, you will have no balance and that can negatively impact your work performance, relationships, spiritual life as well as your health.

Last, you may have been assigned and God-ordained to cover a leader for a specific season of the leader's life, your life, or both. If you are an individual who is called to ministry, the Lord can use this season to drop your leader's mantle on you. Mantles are caught, they are not taught. You must be around the leader to receive it. Often, serving in this capacity is one way that impartation takes place. You may not do exactly what your leader does, but often, there is a gifting that he or she has which the Lord is passing to you. This is why it is so crucial to serve with your whole heart. Since God is faithful to the faithful, you want to sow good seed because you want to reap good seed. You want to be the type of servant you want to be served by. The leader I served preached a message called "Giant Killers." In this message, he made a point which I had never seen in the" David story." He said that David was successful because he had a mental edge over Goliath. Basically he taught that David's mental edge gave him a formula that helped him defeat his enemy. This same mental edge gave David another truly amazing ability: "David had an ability to serve someone sitting in his seat." David was able to serve Saul. Not only did he serve Saul, David honored him by dealing with him respectfully. When Saul tried to give David his armor. He respectfully declined. I love this and it something that we need more of in the kingdom today. If you know the "Saul and David story," David continued to serve Saul and to defend him even when Saul turned on David and began trying to kill him. You have to learn to do what my dear friend Pastor Phil Mitchell calls, "Leaving a dishonorable situation with an honorable exit." When the season ends, it doesn't mean the relationship has to end poorly. You should not burn bridges unless, it necessary. If someone makes it clear that they do not want to retain the relationship and they mistreat you or reject you, then it is smart for you to go on to your next destination. Keep it kingdom, and keep it civilized (as my husband would say). Shake the dust off your feet and keep on moving. That advice is only for situations that truly warrant it. If at all possible, you should leave amicably with the relationship intact. Any other action is not only unwise it is also not biblical. God placed you where you were for a season, and you have to be determined to give thanks, as the old folks would say, "in season and out of season." This "thanksgiving" is often the key to your getting to the next place which God has for you. Learn how to embrace seasons and the changes that they bring. God will never lead you wrong. He knows the end from the beginning. He has you covered and your leader too. You will both "see the goodness of the Lord in the land of the living." Just serve faithfully until your season comes to an end.

Know Your Role Reflection Time

1. In what areas do you need to do a better job of anticipating your leader's needs?

_____

_____

_____

_____

2. How can you "know/flow/go" better with your leader?

_____

_____

_____

_____

3. What do you need to do to create a better communication strategy with your leader? If you need more clarity to complete this task, with whom do you need to talk?

_____

_____

_____

_____

4. How do you handle problems? What can you do to become more solution-oriented? Is there an area that you need to apply this to more than others' (e.g. work, family, etc.)?

_____

_____

_____

_____

5. Are you a drama queen or king? How can you eliminate negativity from your life?

_____

_____

_____

_____

_____

6. Personal Assessment:

A. How are you doing in the area of being prepared for your leader?

_____

_____

_____

_____

_____

B. Into which category do you fall regarding your administration?

_____ *Short-Term/Temporary*

_____ *Ministry Lifer (Career Admin)*

_____ *Long-Term/Seasonal*

C. Create a plan to function at your highest level, depending on your category. *(For example, if you are lifer, you may need to decide the best time of year to take vacation and who will relieve you/or schedule your time while your leader takes his or her vacation if you can.)*

_____

_____

_____

_____

_____

_____

_____

_____

_____

_____

Chapter 5: Knowledge Component #5

Know the Benefits of Serving

To really understand the benefits of serving, we must first eliminate the myths that surround this gift. It is completely possible for something to be more positive than negative but not necessarily be seen in that positive light because of the way that it most often portrayed. Many things are like that. For instance, we are in a presidential election year. As poorly as the candidates have been portrayed on both sides, politics itself is not entirely a bad thing. Several groups of people in the United States had to protest to receive the right to vote. We must dispel the myth that our personal feelings about the people who are running for office override the sacrifice of our ancestors who fought for everyone to have the same rights in this democratic process. We cannot afford to think in that way.

Another area frequently misrepresented is marriage. The way marriage is depicted in media leaves much to be desired. It is not a surprise to me that so many people are not interested in pursuing a committed and monogamous covenant relationship. The irony is that many people are already functioning as husbands and wives every day, but just without the benefits that come along with the rings and the paperwork. One or both of the individuals in those relationships have settled upon the idea that marriage is not necessary, which means they probably do not understand marriage the way that God intended. They have subscribed to a series of myths that render them unable to complete the sacrifice of covenant.

In the same way, if you are going to serve in ministry, you have to make a decision to fully commit. You cannot be lukewarm in "matters of the kingdom." You have to be "all in." I was taught that it is "kingdom first," not "kingdom only," so balance is still an important key to serving. My point is that "serving" has to be something that you are committed to doing, because it isn't something to be taken lightly.

Some of the main reasons that people are unable to commit to serving, is unfortunately due to the fact that much of what is believed about serving in the kingdom is not true at all.

To paraphrase, George Orwell: some myths "are more equal than others." With your gracious permission, I would like to clear up a few of them.

Debunking Serving Myths

Myth # 1: Serving means that you allow yourself to be a slave or a doormat.

If you find yourself in a situation that feels like servitude then you need to check what you are doing, why you are doing it and for whom you are doing it. The Lord asks us to serve, but He doesn't expect us to subject ourselves to abuse or misuse of power or oppression of any kind. I know many people who don't want to have anything to do with church or church leaders because they were abused. There are more ways that you can be oppressed at a church other than physically, mentally or emotionally. For example, you should never feel as though you are in a ministry or church that you cannot leave. Seasons change, and seasons end. If you ever find yourself at a church that is telling you that you can't leave, that is scary and cause for alarm. Because any church that you "cannot" leave is not a church; it is a cult. If that is the case, you should leave and never return. You cannot live that way, and God doesn't intend for you to.

Myth # 2: You shouldn't care what your leaders think.

If you are serving somewhere and you don't care what your leaders think, then you don't value or respect them. If you are in a house where you don't value or respect your leaders, you are in the wrong place. The danger with staying in the wrong place is that often it leads to rebellion and the Word says that "rebellion is as witchcraft." Often, people arrive at this point when a leader or fellow member has wronged them. Even if that is the case, it would still be better for you to leave rather than for you to open the door for the enemy to cause you to begin to operate in rebellion. There are plenty of other places in which you may serve. If you cannot serve in this house, then either you should just attend and not serve or find somewhere that you can do both—serve and attend.

Myth # 3: It is okay for you to serve all the time and never attend service.

This is one of the most serious myths in the church world. We live in such a "social" environment, that church can easily become a "hang out." Church can become a cool place to see all your friends, and if you are not careful, you can find yourself spiritually cold because you are near the fire, but you never go inside to get be warmed by it (figuratively). It is vital that you balance your service with regularly attending worship service and hearing the Word. One of the trage-dies of people who work in full-time ministry is that they become so busy "working" and "serving" at church that every other area of their life can fall apart. Good leaders will bring this deficiency to those individuals' attention, but often the leaders cannot/do not police it for various reasons. If you are a team leader or pastor, I urge you to make sure that you are following up with your staff, top servers, and volunteer staff to ensure that they are getting fed regularly.

Myth # 4: Serving is a way to become "besties" with the Pastors.
Actually, most people will never really be friends with the pastor. It's an "Up" Relationship (see Chapter 2).

Many types of relationships exist within the ministry. Some are more complex than others. One of the most complex can be the relationship between a pastor and the leaders and volunteers who serve the closest with the pastor. Some lead/senior pastors only pastor their pastors, and then they expect those pastors to pastor the leaders and the members. Other pastors (often in smaller churches or when churches are just beginning) pastor/shepherd lead everyone. No matter what type of leadership your church functions under, one thing must be clear—your pastor is not your friend. A good pastor cares about you, prays for you, gives guidance and nurtures you, but one thing a pastor generally is not and that is your friend.

Earlier, we talked about the different types of relationships. The following serves as a good example of an "up" relationship. Now, there are a few exceptions to this rule. If you are blood related to the pastor, grew up with the pastor, knew the pastor before he/she was your pastor you may actually have a "friend" type relationship, but just expect that more than likely the relationship will change over time.

As people who "serve" our leaders, we are here to make their lives better. In a healthy relationship, leaders make our lives better too, just in a different way.

One of the most important reasons to shift this line of thinking is that when "friending" the pastor is the primary motive for serving and that friendship doesn't develop, the individual who has been serving often leaves. When this person leaves, he or she often leaves hurt, angry and feeling "used." So it becomes the equivalent of a bad breakup, and often this person backslides or leaves church altogether, never realizing that even though the task was serving the leader, the assignment was *serving God*. We serve God through our care of our pastors and the visions entrusted to them. It is important for everyone on the team to know this, accept it, and help others realize it, too. This attitude will prevent a great deal of headache later and even save a soul or keep one from becoming lost.

Myth # 5: Everyone can serve.

This is the last myth I want to debunk: many are called, but the chosen are few. Everyone is not called to serve, and everyone cannot serve in the same capacity. I want to urge you all to take a spiritual gifts test. There are several different ones, but they all are basically alike. If you are someone who feels called to work/serve in ministry, it would be beneficial for you to find out what your chief gifts are and to work in those areas.

One of the reasons that everyone can't serve is that serving requires one word that has almost become a curse word in our modern world— that word is <u>sacrifice</u>. This willing act is not something that brings you a great deal of wealth by the general population's standards. That does not change the fact that the rewards are gratifying. The bible tells us that money answers all things, but the older you get, you find out that there is something that you need equally as much and in some instances, more than money. That one thing is favor, and this special blessing is one of the greatest benefits of serving. Serving sets you up for supernatural favor. I served my last leader for five years. At the end of that time, I had served him so long until I had caught my portion of his mantle. When people hear me speak, many say that my ministry communication style is similar to his. Well, before I worked for him on staff, I served as team leader three years prior to that on the Media presentation team, which is the team responsible for putting the sermon notes on the screens. Now, the sacrifice to be on that team is "no joke." I actually can count one hand the numbers of Wednesdays (mid-week services) and Sundays that I missed while I was serving on that team. I came to church sick because there was no one else to run the screens, but what I gained was much greater than what I sacrificed.

That volunteer role opened the door for my full-time positions, which allowed me the opportunity to "make my leader a cake first." If you are not familiar with the story of Elijah and the widow in I Kings 17, I suggest that you take some time to read it in its entirety. It actually is one of my favorite stories in the bible.

I'll give you a quick synopsis to illustrate my point.

Elijah was instructed by God to go to a specific widow's house. We will pick up the story in verse 10.

10 So he went to Zarephath. When he came to the town gate, a widow was there gathering sticks. He called to her and asked, "Would you bring me a little water in a jar so I may have a drink?"

The widow woman was requested to give Elijah a few things. One of the things was not an issue for her: He asked her for water, which she had no problem retrieving. The next request was a bit of an issue. Actually, it was a really big issue because the famine in the land had reached "her house." The issues which were once raging outside her door had made its way <u>inside</u> her house.

11 As she was going to get it, he called, "And bring me, please, a piece of bread." 12 "As surely as the Lord your God lives," she replied, "I don't have any bread—only a handful of flour in a jar and a little olive oil in a jug. I am gathering a few sticks to take home and make a meal for myself and my son, that we may eat it—and die."

This woman had a major problem. Not only did she have a food issue, she had a faith issue. Unknown to her, God had sent Elijah her way to deal with both issues. Therefore, Elijah was not moved by her crisis of faith. He then gave her more exact instructions:

13 Elijah said to her, "Don't be afraid. Go home and do as you have said. But first make a small loaf of bread for me from what you have and bring it to me, and then make something for yourself and your son. 14 For this is what the Lord, the God of Israel, says: 'The jar of flour will not be used up and the jug of oil will not run dry until the day the Lord sends rain on the land.'"

So Elijah responds to her with a Word. He has a prophesy for her. She had a choice. She chose to look beyond what "it looked like" and to trust the man of God and the God in the man of God.

15 She went away and did as Elijah had told her. So there was food every day for Elijah and for the woman and her family. 16 For the jar of flour was not used up and the jug of oil did not run dry, in keeping with the word of the Lord spoken by Elijah.

So not only did her sacrifice reverse the death sentence that she proclaimed on herself and her son, the sacrifice also resulted in her becoming the only food store in town. She became a business owner, and her business was blessed because she had no competition in her town. Everyone had to come to her and to get the ingredients to be fed. Her sacrifice turned into supernatural favor and set her up for God-ordained wealth.

No matter who talks about you for serving, no matter who tries to tell you "It don't take all that," just be sure to continue to make your leader a cake first. The blessings that follow you as a result will follow you all the days of your life.

Lastly, if you serve someone and you don't reap the reward of your serving his or her, don't worry. God's Word cannot be mocked. Whatever you sow, you will reap. Just because you don't reap it in that place doesn't mean you will never reap it. Trust me, (in this instance) God's delay is never His denial. What you don't receive in that place, you will reap it in the next. That's why you must never become weary in your well doing. You will reap a harvest if you faint not. Don't faint. Don't let anyone talk you out the favor that God has designed for you to receive as a result of your serving your leader as unto HIM.

Know the Benefits Reflection Time

What is one of the serving myths that you struggle with today?

_____

_____

_____

_____

Do any of these myths apply to people who are close to you? If so, write down who and which ones.

_____

_____

_____

Read the story of the Elijah and the widow in its entirety. (1 Kings 17)

What revelation do you get out of the story that you can apply to your own life?

_____

_____

_____

_____

Your serving will set you up for supernatural favor. Make a list of areas where you need God to give you favor. Review them and add them to your prayer time.

_____

_____

_____

_____

Are you worshipping and receiving the Word at least twice a month? If not, who can you talk to and what adjustments can be made to make sure you are?

_____

_____

_____

_____

Prayer Time:

Take a moment and pray over the areas that you have listed above that you need supernatural favor.

I am adding my faith to yours that God will bring them to pass for you.

Chapter 6: Knowledge Component #6

Know Your Core Competency

One of the things that I learned very early in life is the value of staying in your own lane. Some of the most successful people I ever met are successful because they are efficient at working their strengths and delegating in their weaknesses. Now, you must be careful because delegating a task to the wrong person only delays the task. Then you get a boomerang effect of the task's coming back to you incomplete and incorrect. However, now you have less time than before to complete the task. So the ability to work in your own lane and build a team around you that can help facilitate you in your weaker areas is an essential component for your kingdom success.

The information I am about to share with you is new. Therefore, for all of you super kingdom admins who are reading the book as a refresher, I want to give you a heads up that this is a fresh download, so be sure to take notes!

One of the most critical components for you is to learn your core competency. If you have ever taken a spiritual-gifts test or a personality test you know that the results of those tests reveal a core or dominant trait. It doesn't mean that you possess only that one, but it is the one which defines you at your core.

It is a lot like compatibility with a significant other. The two of you have to have a common core in order to have a successful relationship. If you try to live with someone whose core is different from yours, you will find yourself in a very contentious, even volatile, situation because you will be at odds about the very thing that is the most important to you.

I once was in a relationship with a guy whose core objective in life was to be rich and live in a mansion. It was not like he did not have other goals, and it was not even like his core objective was a bad one. It just happened to be near the bottom of my list. I grew up in a very nice, spacious, but modest dwelling, and I wanted something similar to that. I wanted a house that I actually could one day pay off in 20 or 25 years, not one that would be anywhere near being paid off when I got ready to go to heaven. As you can imagine, that was a point of severe adversity because when something is central to your core, it drives all of your other actions. It actually colors and shapes how you see the world and all of the aspects of it.

In the same way, I have been serving in the kingdom for precisely 20 years at the time of this writing in 2016. I was raised in church and have been involved in church my entire life, but at 19, I led my first ministry. It was a liturgical dance ministry for children ages 4-12. I still remember those rehearsals. They were a nightmare, but we got through them, and the first songs I ever taught them were all on the Kirk Franklin God's Property album (to prove to you all how long ago it was)! Since then, I have served in the following areas:

- Liturgical Dance Team Leader & Dancer (Adult Ministry)
- Graphic & Layout Designer
- Web & Content Maintenance Manager
- Administrative Assistant
- Executive Director

- Content Development Manager
- Marketing Administrator
- Brand Manager
- Writer
- Editor
- Social Media Manager
- Travel Coordinator
- Public Relations Manager
- Executive Assistant to the Senior Pastor

As I was preparing for Component number 6 to be something entirely different, I began to reflect on serving in all of these capacities. I realized that there are 6 primary capacities that exist, and one of them is serves as your core. You probably have a secondary core strength, but for now, we will just focus on your discovering the one that is your core competency—your driving force.

I made them all start with C's because I hang out with preachers, and I learned this cool trick from them: It helps you remember lists when they all start with the same letter (alliteration for all the English majors).

1. **Clerical/Project Management**—If your core competency is clerical or project management, you are probably slightly obsessive compulsive with the details. You need details about the details. You need updates, to-do lists and the more meetings, the better. You are someone who is more project-focused than people focused. You will run over the people if they get in the way of marking the checklist off. The good news is that we cannot do kingdom without the clerical, project management people. The benefits of this core strength is that you are driven to get tasks completed, and with you in the picture, they are more likely to get executed with accuracy, swiftness, and precision. You ask the

questions that no one thinks of, and you hold every single person accountable for every task, every dollar, and every minute it takes to get it done. The drawback to this core strength is that people can get knocked around and trampled by the methods with which this core is carried out. So if this is you, make sure that you have people around you who can handle your people tenderly while you are checking off the lists. Over time, if you can, try to strike a balance between your assertive, tenacious go-getter spirit to achieve the results and working with the team to make sure that you are communicating in a way that is as "wise as a serpent, but harmless as a dove." If you are just driven and niceties are a struggle with you, just make sure you keep people around you who can be a buffer and can give the people warm fuzzies while you monitor and execute the objectives. This is critical, crucial, and key when you are working with volunteers. Remember that volunteers are not paid staff. They are giving up their time freely to assist you with your kingdom tasks, so be sure that they always feel valued and appreciated—even during crunch time when no-joke tasks have to be completed.

2.   **Communication**—If communication is your CORE competency you are the person who is efficient at making sure that everyone knows what is going on. You are making sure—by any means necessary—phone call; text message; Facebook message; Twitter/Instagram direct message; Google hangout; freeconferencecall.com, skype or smoke signals (just kidding) that you communicate with your team. You understand that communication is a precious commodity in the kingdom. You understand that a service or event can be amazing or a "hot mess," based on the communication plan or lack thereof of all the players involved. The benefit of this core competency is that

you are a "glue" in your organization. You help fix things that are broken as well as keep things from breaking. Your value is priceless, especially the larger or busier a church is. You make sure that the right people get copied on emails. You see when a call is needed instead of a text. You are the person who follows up when a mass text is sent and someone doesn't respond. You pay attention to communicative details. This is a crucial and critical skill as an administrator. Communication-core individuals are not only superb at these skills, but they pay attention to the communication skills of others. They can tell you the best way to reach out to a group of people. They know that they need to send a follow-up email to the administrative assistants after sending an email to the pastoral staff because they make mental notes of who reads his or her email. They learn the best times to communicate with certain individuals. They note times that they are successful reaching those people, and they remember for the next time. Communication-core individuals are invaluable assets to assist with Public Relations. They understand the power of storytelling and know how to help leaders connect with the community. Communicators naturally connect people, places, ideas and events.

Communicators and Social Media

Speaking of natural connections, you are also a great person to assist with social media. Social Media is not going anywhere, and it would greatly benefit the church to be active on Facebook, Instagram, and YouTube, to name a few. In a media world that is constantly changing, someone in your organization has to keep up with the digital, tech and communication trends and ensure that they are be explored and then executed within your local church body. Social Media helps younger generations identify and even qualify your church as a "real brand." We discuss generational mindsets in a later chapter, but for now, just know that if your church is going to thrive in today's world, it will not be able to do without a digital footprint. Now, the only downside to the communication-core is that you can often lose time because, generally, people with this gift like to talk. They like to share information, and sometimes they can unknowingly end up connected to gossipers and drama queens/kings because they, too, are communicators. The difference is that you use your gift for good and not evil, and they, unfortunately, mostly use the gift for ill. I caution you to be mindful of the company you keep and attract. Last, I encourage you to use social media as the blessing I believe it was intended to be to the body of believers. Share good experiences that you have at your church, and encourage others to do the same. Use the "invite tools" to invite others to events. Occasionally, "go live" on video (Facebook/Periscope), and give others a taste of the worship experience at your church. In the end, as a communicator, you have the opportunity to help your ministry go to the next level through digital evangelism. Make sure you tap into your gift!

Communicators and Content Management

Communicators also are efficient in helping pastors and leaders with sermons, sermon notes, content development, and book creation. Another downside to being a communication-core is that this is such a time-consuming core that it can make you lag behind in other areas. Be sure to build a support team around you to assist in the other areas so that you can soar in this area without any other balls getting dropped.

3. **Creative**—If your core is creative, then most likely, communication is your secondary core strength. Often, these two work

closely together. Creative-core individuals process information differently than the other Core-strength groups. Creative-core people see everything as an opportunity to make something better. They always see "another way to skin the cat." They are often masterful at compromise because they are gifted in seeing so many multiple ways to achieve an objective that they apply communication skills (knowing what everyone is trying to achieve) that figure out "win-win" scenarios in various types of situations.

Creatives care about how things look. They are keenly mindful of the five senses. They are helpful in pointing out when something smells bad, when the environment feels off, or when a visual component is lacking. They also learn when the audio is functioning improperly or is too loud. Creatives tend to be tunnel-visioned like communication-core individuals, so the same advice is given to them as communication-core individuals: build a team around you that is efficient or has core strengths in the areas you do not. If you do not do this, over time you will find the other tasks mundane and increasingly more difficult to do. If your ministry cannot afford staff to assist, find some volunteers, and enlist their support. Your work will suffer over time in the other areas if you do not proactively get assistance.

Creatives often dabble in graphics, interior design, and all hands-on visual and artistic elements of ministry. They often have superior imaginations and are very effective in transforming spaces and assisting with Communication-core with content and social media imagery.

4. **Corporate**—If your core is corporate, you are saved, and you may love your church, but you see the business side of church just as much as you see the church as a fellowship and life-changing entity. If you are corporate, your secondary core maybe clerical/project management, for these cores are similar. If you are

corporate, you see the church through the lens of possible audits, budgets, and projected income. You may help with business development and see the opportunities for the church to diversify its income so that it is not just solely dependent upon tithes and offerings. You may have an MBA, or you may have some other sort of business, finance or C-level executive *(CEO, COO, i.e.)* experience or background. You are so needed in the church. Sometimes, we are quite advanced at service planning and bad at financial planning and management. The only downfall to your core is that you may struggle if the leader is led to do something that cannot be backed by a feasibility study. You may have a hard time justifying a mission trip when you feel the money could be better spent serving communities locally. You must seek God and ask for peace in these circumstances. For you, more than any other core—you must completely trust God and your leader. If you don't, it can be easy for you to become frustrated with not just the church you currently attend, but any church. The truth is that when you see ministry through a corporate lens, your perspective can be "If it doesn't make dollars, then it doesn't make sense." However, a visionary always trusts that "little becomes much when it is put in the Master's hands." That may be a tough pill for you to swallow (figuratively), but an essential one.

The other downside to your core is that just like the Clerical/project management, you, too, can be project-driven over people-focused. You can end up damaging someone in ministry because you were "doing your job." You, too, need buffer people around you to help if you struggle in those areas. Just know that we need your gift; we need checks and balances to help keep us all together. We need that business perspective so that the church cannot only thrive but survive.

5. **Collaborative**—If your core competency is collaborative, you are skilled at bringing people together, you are a gatherer of people and a builder of teams. You pay attention to people. You get to know people. You are a networker and a bridge builder. This is an essential Core that every administrator needs to have or possess. This is a very unique Core to have but is a gift that all administrators would be wise to learn. This is the only core-competency that I believe can be grasped and mastered over time. Because no man is an island, collaboration is essential in the kingdom. It is so crucial that you can be eliminated from a team if the leaders feel that you cannot function in this capacity, regardless of what your Core is. So if you are an individual who likes to work alone, just know that for the sake of kingdom work, you will have to step out of your bubble, even if it is just occasionally, to be a part of the larger group. Eventually, a situation will arise where collaboration will be non-negotiable.

6. **Community**—If your Core is community you are "all things to all people." You are compassionate. You have sympathy and empathy for others. You want to show people the goodness of God through service and helping others in every way imaginable. Community-core individuals often have a secondary-core of collaboration. You understand that it takes team work to be a blessing to the masses. Also, you are relationship-focused and are instantly attracted to like-minded people who have the same objectives as you do. The only downside to community is that you tend to think that the ministry should be doing more. You may think that more of the resources should be going to community resources. Just know that even though helping others is essential to the mission, there must be a budget by which to keep everything running. I once was in a staff meeting in which the

executive pastor reminded us that there was one pie. He told us that if he did not monitor the pie slices going out, then someone would go without because everyone had to get fed from that one pie. I thought that was an excellent example. Although it was years ago, I never have forgotten it. The truth is that wherever your core is, your heart is also. Thus, communication-core people want a large piece of the pie to go to social media and PR training and events; creative people want to spend the pie on cameras, lights, and remodeling. Community-core people are not entirely different from others, but often the intensity is significantly different because when your ministry builds a habitat for humanity house and you meet the person who is going to live there, you might feel as though everyone in the church should donate time to that cause. As a warning, just know that everyone is not going to be as passionate or compassionate about community as you. That, my friend is okay, because we have you!

Super Kingdom Admin Core Competency Assignment

1. Based on reading the material above, rank the competencies in the order that you think they apply to you. Mark your first Core competency, followed by your secondary core and so on. If you get to a core that you think doesn't apply to you at all, write N/A for not applicable.

    Rank:

    ___ Clerical

    ___ Communication

    ___ Creative

    ___ Corporate

    ___ Collaborative

    ___ Community

2. Write your core competency here _____.

3. Write the core that applies to you the least_____.

Now provide yourself an action plan of person(s) you need around you to support the areas where you are not as strong.

_____

_____

_____

_____

_____

_____

List one member of your team you can hold accountable to complete the action plan above.

_____

List the most valuable concept/principle you learned from this section.

_____

_____

If collaboration is not your core, and doesn't come easy to you, what are some ways that you can work on integrating it into your admin life? List some people who do admin so well that you would like to work with them. Consider what benefits you would gain from working with them.

_____

_____

_____

_____

Core Prayer:

Lord, thank you for revelation of learning how you strategically assigned and specifically designed me to serve in Your kingdom. Please strengthen me in the areas I am weak and send committed, loyal people to serve alongside me. Lord, I thank you in advance for calling me and equipping for service in Your kingdom, for Your people. I am determined to help my leaders and my church reach as many souls for you as I can by using my core competencies and strengths. Thank you for wisdom and knowledge in Jesus Name I pray, Amen.

Chapter 7: Knowledge Component #7

Know the State of the Kingdom

Two types of people generally make up church membership—the "churched" and the "un-churched/non-churched."

The *churched* group actually grew up going to church and attending services and religious events. This group has different levels within it:

1. First are individuals who attended church, but did not get anything out of it. They went only because they were made to go.

2. Second are people who went to church and believed in God at an early age, but strayed and then returned to God later in life. Usually, some life-changing event or series of bad choices has created a crisis that has driven them back to the church.

3. Then there is the last group; those who grew up in church, believed in God early and have been in church (and maintained his or her relationship with God). This group seems to be a continuously decreasing population.

The un-churched category is made up of individuals who are introduced to God or organized religion/church later in life.

However, another shift is trending right now—the community church within the megachurch. Right now, some of the largest churches in our nation have satellite campuses. The main church campus may seat anywhere from 2,000-4,000 congregants, but the satellite or community church sites are designed to accommodate much smaller congregations. The majority of the latter seat around 500 congregants, and they typically are no larger than 1,000 congregants.

So many of the larger churches who have not embraced this model are losing members who desire that community feeling and personal touch. The larger churches who are still thriving are doing so with small groups, intentional event planning and "keeping their finger on the pulse" of their congregation and its changing needs.

The needs are certainly changing as the generations mature.

Generation Z (iGen/Gen-Z) Born: 2020-2000

Generation Y (Millennials) Born: 2002-1982

Generation X Born: 1980-1960

Boomers Born: 1964-1946

It is important to understand that not only are millennials a part of the modern church, but also a new generation is growing up that the church will have to be prepared to minister to as well: Gen-Z (see the chart above).

Gen-Zers are far less optimistic than their Millennial counter-parts. They have grown up post-9/11, and they are one of the most pessimistic, non-trusting generations we have ever seen. Gen-Zers will need to be convinced of something to believe in (and it will be difficult for both the churched and the non-churched). Leaders must also be aware that this is a group that will have to believe in the Messenger as much as the message. They struggle with anything that is not branded and not easily found online, so the messaging will need to be powerful and impactful from the start. The generation before

Gen-Z has a much better outlook, as the Millennials are considerably more optimistic. However, those in this group have the weight of the world on their shoulders. For example, they will probably be the first generation responsible for their own retirement funds (with every generation losing confidence in the government's social security system), so they, too, need to be inspired and encouraged.

Both Generation X and Baby Boomers are easier to reach, in most cases, and easier to minister to if they have not been the victims of church hurt or severely unmet church expectations. More of them are familiar with church, which can be a positive or negative, depending on the experiences they have had. Baby Boomers generally are the largest giving group, even though Generation X is noted as the first generation to be as highly educated across the entire generation (with more secondary degrees than any generation previously), they still do not give the amounts as the generation who precedes them. Gen Xers and Millennials are more self-absorbed than the Boomers, which makes them, in many instances, a more consuming Christian culture than giving. These facts could be a major contributing factor as to why both the Millennials and Gen-Z are also not widespread believers in "tithes and offerings," but they are givers. This is important to know because it will impact how the church functions financially in the years to come. A light is at the end of the tunnel, nevertheless. Although the younger generations are not as quick to give regularly in offerings or become tithers, they do, in fact, give. They are considered "cause" givers, though.

They will donate their time, talent, and treasure to a worthy cause. If there is a catastrophe, not only will they give to it, but they also will buy a plane ticket and go assist on the ground. So churches will have to be involved in community empowerment, and it must be evident and clear "what" the funds are being used for, and "who" their funds are benefiting, as the younger generations are not giving out a sense of obligation or tradition.

Keep in mind that in addition to being a generation that consists of large numbers, many were and are being raised by a single mother. These generations are the first no-parent generation, as many of them were sent to live with grandparents and other relatives as large numbers of abandoned children were left by parents (not generally intentionally) because of drug use and incarceration, especially for minorities as longer sentences have been issued in the last several decades. According to the American Civil Liberties Union, women are the fastest growing segment of the incarcerated population, increasing at nearly double the rate of men since 1985. Over the past twenty years, the war on drugs has caused a significant rise in the number of women incarcerated, and the judicial system started locking up women who were the wives and girlfriends of drug dealers, and giving them maximum minimums. In some states, the rate of sentencing among woman has gone up as high as 800 percent in the last twenty years. Two-thirds of state female prisoners have a minor child; consequently someone is left to raise these children.

Over 1.5 million children have a parent in prison. This may not seem like a big deal, but these children grow up being raised by family members, in and out of foster care, or being raised by adopted parents. Some of the situations turn out well, but many of them do not. These children are more likely to be victims of physical and sexual crimes. They are more likely to become a teen parent. They are more susceptible to gang activity, drug activity, or drug/alcohol abuse. Therefore, it is important to understand how the social ills of society affect the people who attend our services every week.

People who group up in these environments develop a survival mentality relatively early. In fact, they really do not have a choice.

So those same "survivor instincts" cause them to be more focused on their personal achievement and advancement than advancing the cause of another organization that they are not personally tied to, like, for example, a fraternity or sorority.

The other major factor of the last two generations is that the ones who are raised with their parents have seen their parents work hard and still be subject to lay-offs and workplace discrimination racially and/or gender-related. As a result, each generation is getting a little less materialistic and instead savvier with money, investments, and savings. The last two generations also have an overly entrepreneurial mindset. They are not as interested in working for someone else. They have issues with authority, especially when they are not certain if those leading them have their best interests at heart.

The role of the church leaders has been made even more difficult with the popularity of reality TV shows. The shows that feature preachers and pastors sometimes do not present those leaders in the best light. Couple the impression left by shows with the personal mistakes and public failings of church leaders in the media, and it has become even more difficult for people of all generations to trust integrity of clergy in the modern church.

Having said all of that, I am compelled to say that the church is in need of a "facelift." It is the responsibility of all believers to live the life we proclaim on Sunday. It must be evident in our conduct, speech and social media that we are servants of the Most-High God and that we live our lives by a different standard.

When I was dating my husband, I was working in the capacity of executive assistant, and our courtship went on long enough for us to be sure that we were "right" for one another. If we had waited longer, I would have had a bigger wedding with more bells and whistles, but I wanted to make sure that we did not fall into sin because we were "waiting to have it all together" before we got married. As a matter of fact, it was far from together. My husband was living in another city and working in another city and he did not want to commute at all, but we made a commitment to God and to each other and it has worked. We don't have it all, but we are both agree that we are the happiest that we have ever been in a relationship in our entire lives. The happiness that we possess shows when people are around us, and reflects that love is an example of the love that God had for believers. It, moreover, is a sacrificial love. We had to give something up to be together, and you will have to give up something to serve well in the kingdom. The kingdom will, in fact, cost you everything, but when you seek the kingdom first, God subsequently adds unto you immeasurably above anything you could ever ask, think, or imagine.

When you make a decision to be a kingdom ambassador, God has no choice but to bless you. Your serving sets you up for supernatural, unexplainable favor to the amazement of both receiver and observer.

That favor will overtake you and the generations that follow you, so never be weary in your well doing. Your serving God and your leaders is so crucial to the kingdom, and it is more crucial than ever before. In a time when people are so consumed with themselves, God is looking for some individuals who are willing to be used. He needs some people who will sacrifice to make His name great. He needs you. Understanding these things and the state of the kingdom is the last key to unlocking your super kingdom powers and obtaining success.

State of the Kingdom Admin Assignment:

How has this chapter helped you see the kingdom differently?

_____

_____

_____

_____

After reading this chapter in what way can you best help your leaders and church?

_____

_____

_____

_____

State of the Kingdom Prayer:

Lord, thank you for using us to advance your kingdom. You have chosen all of us, for such a time as this, to lift Your name and draw all people to You. Please strengthen us during these challenging times and help us to always focus on the assignment You have given to us. We know that the harvest is plentiful, but the laborers are few. We commit to using our resources and revelation we receive to uplift of Your Name. Amen.

Chapter 8

Super Kingdom Admin Conclusion

I pray that the 7 components have been a blessing to you and have helped you to see kingdom more clearly and the value of your role as an administrator and a Believer in the body of Christ.

In my conclusion, I would like to give you a bonus knowledge component.

1 But know this, that in the last days perilous times will come: 2 For men will be lovers of themselves, lovers of money, boasters, proud, blasphemers, disobedient to parents, unthankful, unholy, 3 unloving, unforgiving, slanderers, without self-control, brutal, despisers of good, 4 traitors, headstrong, haughty, lovers of pleasure rather than lovers of God, 5 having a form of godliness but denying its power. And from such people turn away! 6 For of this sort are those who creep into households and make captives of gullible women loaded down with sins, led away by various lusts, 7 always learning and never able to come to the knowledge of the truth.

2 Timothy 3:1-7

The last few thoughts I would like to leave with you are:

Be persistent about knowing the mission of your church.

Every church has an assignment. Every leader who is following God receives a vision from Him. The leader's vision should be interwoven in the fabric of the mission of your church. Different churches have different missions. I have served in churches that were very event-focused. Those churches were great at evangelism because people often came in to be entertained and left arrested under the power of the Holy Spirit. Some churches are global-mission focused, and those churches are responsible for changing lives around the world. Other churches have a strong connection to the community and serve underprivileged populations of people. Some of these churches have tutoring programs, summer camps, and before-and-after school drop-offs at affordable costs. Last, some churches at their nucleus are about restoration and life improvement. These churches may work with homeless shelters, domestic abuse victims, or offer vocational programs for ex-offenders. No matter what the core mission of your church is, you need to know it and be fervent about helping your leader fulfill it.

The verse in Timothy above gives a blue print for what the last days look like. We are experiencing a great deal of that right now. People need to be able to see something different when they come to church. The church needs a "facelift." It looks a lot like the world, and we have been warned to be in the world and not of it. So make sure you that are a part of the team that makes the mission of your church clearly defined. That way you are not just helping your church; you are helping the entire Body of Christ.

Make sure that lives are truly being changed.

As previously stated, we are in the "people business." If the agenda being pushed is not making a difference in the lives of the people we serve, we must evaluate whether it truly lines up with the mandate of the church outlined in the scriptures. As an administrator, you may not have the authority to overturn a concept that is currently in motion, but you have an obligation to use your influence in a **godly and non-manipulative** manner to make suggestions and assist the leaders with the decisions that affect the people. You should never openly rebuke an idea or concept given by a leader. Through prayer and leading of the Holy Spirit, you should offer such feedback in a humble and gracious manner as a suggestion and never as a command or challenge. You should always be harmless as a dove. Never forget that God has put you in that place at this time for such a season. Your voice could usher in a movement. As you spend more time with your leader, you will know best how and when to approach him or her. With God on your side, through prayer and supplication, you will be able to make suggestions in a helpful, non-threatening, non-disrespectful way. Remember that the longer you serve, the more your leader will lean on your judgement, wisdom and discernment, so you must stay prayerful so that you can assist him or her in a non-biased and purely spirit-led, yet educated manner. I know that I continue to stress it, but I feel a strong urge to make sure that I clearly articulate this to you. Many people are connected to the leader, some of whom allow their influence to lead the leader in a way that causes negative results. People who use their influence for evil or personal gain have no place in the kingdom. The Lord allows a season for such individuals to repent before He intervenes, so please, please always make sure that your motives are pure before you present anything to your leader. Anything else is unfair, unjust, and dishonorable to God, your leader, the people you all serve, yourself, and to the position that you have been entrusted to fulfill.

Be sure that people know God better.

The worse two things that can happen to your members are that either they never change and live a bad life or that they use church as a "fix," a temporary high from their bad lives. Neither of these experiences is good.

If your church members do not know God better after worshipping and fellowshipping within your local body, something is wrong. If people come in heathens and leave out as heathens (unchanged, unrepentant) week after week, someone will need to desperately make some adjustments. The modern church is a spectacular place, but we have to be diligent to make sure that it doesn't become a spectacle. The lights, the sound system, and the screens are all appealing, but it can't just be merely a good 90-minute show or social gathering. We have to make sure that our people are experiencing God, and not just using church as a drug or temporary escape from their personal lives. When people know God better, their lives are better. We must become intentional about messages and methodologies that help people not only be excited about a good life in Heaven, but also have a good life here on Earth.

Be sure that you are spreading the word about your church and invite others to church.

I have been taught that the number one reason people come to church is because they were invited by someone to attend. Think of your church as a restaurant. Imagine in this restaurant that you are one of the chefs or a part of the wait staff. I know people who work at restaurants while they are in college, or even as a part-time job. Only one of those people has ever invited me to the restaurant where he or she worked. I can only imagine that all of those restaurant employees trust the commercials, ads, or billboards to direct the people to the restaurant, but the truth of the matter is that marketing is everyone's responsibility. If people ever stop coming to the restaurant, there would be no one to cook for and no orders to take. It is everyone's job to invite people to worship and fellowship at your church.

In closing, I want you to know that you are essential to the kingdom-building process. I have been fortunate enough to travel quite a bit as I have begun sharing this message, and there is something that I have never seen. I have never seen a pilot leave the cockpit and pass out blankets and serve drinks. That says to me that the flight attendants have an important job. If the pilot has to do anything other than fly the plane, every life on the plane is in danger.

In the same way, God has entrusted you to take care of the pilot and the people on board. Don't be weary in your well doing. You shall indeed reap a harvest if you faint not. Never forget that you are a super kingdom admin and that you have been empowered with everything you need to achieve success and help your leaders obtain it as well.

May God bless you and keep you and heaven shine upon you.

Until we meet again…be blessed.

Final Super Kingdom Admin Action Items:

1. **Learn your church's mission. If you don't know it, schedule a time to discuss it with your leader. If you already know it, list it here:**

   _____

   _____

   _____

   _____

   _____

2. **In what ways does your church help people know God better? In what ways do you think your church could better administer this help?**

   _____

   _____

   _____

   _____

3. **List three people that you will invite to church in the next 30 days. (If you already are diligent in inviting people to church, list three people who you can witness to about receiving Christ as their Savior).**

   1. _____

   2. _____

   3. _____

Closing Prayer:

Lord, I am grateful for the opportunity to serve in your kingdom. I thank you for the leaders you have entrusted me to help. Please let me see the vision of my leader and the mission of my church clearly. Please give me a boldness to witness to others in these last and evil days. Thank you for the revelation and wisdom that I have received. I pray that you help me to apply it to myself and teach it to others. Amen.

Special Note & Thanks

First, I thank God for saving me, redeeming and delivering me from the snare of the enemy. I don't look like what I have been through, and I have been through fire. But I don't smell like smoke. I thank God that He rescued me and saw fit to use me, in spite of me. I pray that every single thing that I attempt to do for the remainder of my days gives Him glory because it truly is in Him that I "live, move and have my being." I am excited, and I fully expect to see the goodness of the Lord in the land of the living. Then, at the appointed time, one glad morning, at the end of my time here on Earth, I hope to hear him say, "Well done, thy good and faithful servant." My prayer is that while I am still on this side of glory that my life will be a blessing to His people and that I will live out my purpose with intentionality and steadfast determination every day.

Special Note & Thanks

I am eternally grateful for my husband Jason Davis. What a man, what man, what a mighty good man! (*Old Salt 'n Pepa song reference*) There really are no words to describe how perfect this man is for me. He is my biggest fan, my toughest critic, but most importantly, he is my very best friend. God truly saved the best for last, and I am so elated that I get to live my long-awaited "happily ever after" with Him!

I would not be here without Gerald & Ruby Simmons who brought me into the world. The Lord knew that I would need elements from them both and carefully crafted my DNA for the assignment He had predestined me to do. They are truly the most supportive, loving, forgiving and long-suffering parents on the planet. I have always felt that I had tremendous advantage in developing my relationship with God because He gave me such faithful parents. It was, therefore, easy for me to have faith and trust in a Faithful God. Good parents make a vibrant relationship with the Lord easy.

I am blessed with an amazing family! My love to all my children— Chynah and Denzel; Rubie; Amirah; Adiyah; Braxton; Jamera, and the latest addition, my grandson, Matthew—the promise of generational blessings, makes me more passionate about using my gifts and helping others use theirs.

The two pastors who put me on this Super Kingdom Admin path were Pastor Andy Thompson (World Overcomers Christian Church) and Pastor Brian Duley (Nikao Church). Pastor Duley hired me to work in a part-time capacity [while he was serving as Executive Pastor at WOCC] after I had volunteered faithfully for over two years. As time passed, Pastor Andy selected me to serve as his Executive Assistant, a position in which I was honored to serve for the last 5 years. These two men changed the trajectory of my life, and their foresight allowed my gifts to make room for me and flourish in each capacity I undertook at WOCC. The connections and lifelong friendships which I have made are priceless, and I will be eternally grateful for their entrusting me to help lead and manage in these capacities.

I am eternally grateful to Pastor Phil & Lady Lena Mitchell (Victory Church ATL). Their desire to equip and empower their volunteer staff and belief in me is the entire reason that the Super Kingdom Admin material exists. The love and support given by them and the entire Victory Church family is appreciated beyond words!

Next, I am sending special thanks to Pastor Ron Simmons (Designers Way), Pastor Colin Morgan (Good Life) and Pastor Howard Harrison (New Beginnings) all of whom have allowed me share and perfect, and promulgate this message in their cities and moreover have convinced me that it needed to be put into a more permanent format.

I am grateful to Dr. Peter and Patricia Morgan who prayed a special blessing over me and this kingdom work after hearing it and to Pastor Dwayne Dawkins (Praise Tabernacle International) for hosting the session.

I also like thank Beverly Robinson (Potters House Dallas) and the C.E.A.S.E. organization (ceaseadmin.com) for their continued commitment to educate and support kingdom administrators. I have been so encouraged and inspired by their leadership!

Apostle Michael and Prophet Annette Branch (Cutting Word Ministries), who always remind me of the call on my life when I need reminding the most.

I am grateful to Pastor Joseph Michael Foster (Outrageous Living), who gave me my first writing project which led me down the path of assisting clergy with their writing projects and eventually led to me penning a book myself.

Last, but not certainly not least, I am grateful for the pastoral staffs, past and present, that I have served along the way in the body of Christ. Each of you, too numerous to name, has taught me valuable lessons, many of them outlined in this book.

Thank you all so much!

Additional References

"Standing in the Need" is an African American spiritual, and, like many folk songs, its origin is unknown. Both text and tune became well known after their publication in *The Book of American Negro Spirituals* (1925), compiled by James Weldon Johnson and his brother,]. Rosamond Johnson.

Living Bible (TLB)

New International Version (NIV)

New King James Version

The Message (MSG)

Generations Broken Down By Age:

http://luckyattitude.co.uk/gen-x-gen-y-gen-z-baby-boomers/

CPSIA information can be obtained
at www.ICGtesting.com
Printed in the USA
BVHW071916140122
626309BV00005B/322